Advance Praise for *Called*

"Casey Cole's new book is an engaging snapshot of the life of a young Franciscan: his hopes and dreams, his daily joys and struggles, and, especially, his relationship with God. Inviting, accessible, and inspirational, it's also a fine introduction to Franciscan spirituality, ever old but ever new."

—James Martin, SJ, author of *The Jesuit Guide to (Almost) Everything*

"Intensely personal yet deeply ecclesial, Casey Cole's story is my story and yours; it is the path of God's pilgrim people. As a brother to Francis of Assisi, who chose poverty in this world, Friar Casey will help reveal the mysterious working of God's grace in your quest to follow the Christ, Who became poor that we might be truly and eternally rich."

—Bishop Robert Reed, CatholicTV Network

"By telling his own story of vocational discernment and initial formation, Casey Cole invites readers to reflect on the various ways God is calling them to say yes to God. This book will be especially helpful for young women and men who are looking for insight from someone who understands personally the challenges of evangelizing in a digital age, while also striving to live the Gospel with sincerity."

—Daniel P. Horan, OFM, Catholic Theological Union (Chicago), author, *Dating God: Live and Love in the Way of St. Francis*

D1016165

"Many people are curious as to what goes into the call to a vocation. Many have heard quick responses but few have had the opportunity to hear what Brother Casey is revealing about the call. He is clear, honest and offers useful insight into this important decision regarding time spent on earth and the impact on eternity. Keep several copies on hand to share with those who may be called but need direction."

—Jeff Cavins, founder, The Great Adventure
Bible Study System

Casey Cole, OFM

called

WHAT HAPPENS AFTER
SAYING YES TO GOD

franciscan
media
Cincinnati, Ohio

Cover design by LUCAS Art & Design
Book design by Mark Sullivan

LIBRARY OF CONGRESS CATALOGING-IN-PUBLICATION DATA
Names: Cole, Casey, author.
Title: Called : what happens after saying yes to God / Casey Cole, OFM.
Description: Cincinnati : Franciscan Media, 2018.
Identifiers: LCCN 2017061472 | ISBN 9781632532411 (trade paper)
Subjects: LCSH: Vocation—Christianity. | Christian life.
Classification: LCC BV4740 .C645 2018 | DDC 248.8/9422--dc23
LC record available at https://lccn.loc.gov/2017061472

ISBN 978-1-63253-241-1

Published by Franciscan Media
28 W. Liberty St.
Cincinnati, OH 45202
www.FranciscanMedia.org

Printed in the United States of America
Printed on acid-free paper
18 19 20 21 22 5 4 3 2

* * * * * *

contents

I

. . . . . .

introduction

Saying Yes Is Only the Beginning

Six years ago, I said yes to God. The culmination of much discernment and prayer over a number of years, I found myself sitting alone in a chapel no longer afraid of what I was going to do with my life. Finally confident in who I was and comfortable with who God wanted me to be, I was ready to begin living completely for God rather than myself. In that chapel so many years ago, I accepted what I believed that meant: I was going to be a Franciscan friar, serving the poor and living in prayerful community for the sake of the kingdom of God.

And I did. The following year, I joined the formation program of the Order of Friars Minor, and six years later, I publicly professed my solemn and lifelong vows to live the rest of my life as a friar. I said yes, and I meant it.

From a certain perspective, I could definitely understand how some might perceive my moment of surrender in that chapel so many years ago as the effective end of my journey of discernment. At the time, I probably would have said so myself. No longer held back by my old sense of self or clouded by an infinite number of possible futures, I was ready to be who God was calling me to be. After my profound and initial yes to God, I could on that day only see my solemn profession as a further formality in cementing what I had already accepted. The tough part was over—I knew what I wanted to do—now all I had to do was live it.

Ha! If only it were that easy.

Almost immediately after joining the friars and all throughout my years of formation, I realized that this was not going to be the case. As much emphasis as I had put in answering the initial question, and as profound as it was for me to accept what God had prepared for me, I have been reminded almost every day since then that saying yes is just the beginning of a life with God. Life did not get easier when I turned my will over as I had expected. No, the journey of faith, to my surprise, became much more difficult.

My guess is that I am not alone in this experience. No, I can actually state with tremendous confidence that I am not alone because this experience is universal to each and every Christian who feels called in the silence of his or her heart to be a disciple of Christ and is inspired to say yes. Accepting the call to go on the journey, no matter how difficult or self-sacrificing it may be, does not guarantee a safe or successful trip. In fact, as a Christian, it most assuredly means that there will be bumps along the road.

Why is that? Why, when we are finally able to turn from our own desires and begin to do what God wants, does God make everything so much more difficult? This question, as frustrating and uninspiring as it is, is the thread that runs through this book. While I have no intention to speculate about the mind of God or explain the ways of our unknowable Mystery, I think that our ability to grapple with this question, to move beyond our initial yes and deal with what comes next, is the most essential task we have if we want to be able to *continue* to say yes with any conviction.

Using my own story as a foundation and means of organization, I have chosen an assortment of my blog posts from the past six years—moments of discernment captured in time—to offer a glimpse of the ups and downs we might experience when we accept this life in Christ. Looking back with the eyes of faith and the wisdom of mentors, I hope to tell a story that not only sheds light on what can happen after we are ready to say yes to God, but to offer insights into how even the struggles and frustrations of this life can be seen as joy when God is our guide and mission is our focus.

This story, although including me and told from my perspective, is truly not *about* me. No, this story is *our* story, the story of discernment and discipleship that we all share as Christians. What I have experienced and struggled with as a Franciscan friar about discernment, prayer, relationships, humility, mission, and failure are not extraordinary in their own right or worthy of following on their own; the point is not to give an account of what it means to be a twenty-first-century Franciscan or so that others will follow the path in a literal way. No, what I have experienced and struggled with in this life is worth telling because it applies to us all, each in our own individual way as Christians.

So, who is the book for then?

There is no question that, just as my blog has served as a resource for those considering religious life for more than six years, this book will be helpful for those looking for a firsthand account of a young religious. Joining religious life today is not the same as it was fifty years ago, and knowing that you are not going about it alone is tremendously reassuring. It is my hope that these reflections will offer insights and inspiration to continue along that path of discernment with a companion by your side.

Similarly, I believe that this book was written for those who look at my life from the outside and are left in puzzlement and suspicion. For those who are not Catholic or are unfamiliar with modern life in religious orders, why would someone so young and able commit himself to such a strange life? Even for those of my fellow brothers and sisters in consecrated life, those who have lived the life I have just begun for many years and know much more than I do, but who may wonder why this younger generation seems to want something different out of it. Why do we wear our habits? Why is faith sharing and intimacy so important to our communal lives? In this way, this book is for all those who may be on the outside looking in, a humble *apologia* for this way of life that means so much to me.

But there is an even more essential audience than the first two: This book is written for any Christian who desires to be a more faithful disciple of Jesus Christ. As much as my specific life as a Franciscan matters to me and I wish to share it with the whole world, at the very core of who I am and what I have experienced is my life as a disciple of Christ. What I share in this book is meant to offer inspiration and guidance to all those discerning a life in Christ, to offer another companion voice on your journey. What you wonder, what you struggle with, what you experience in your daily life... you do not experience alone.

All Christians must discern God's call for them.

All Christians struggle at times with knowing how to pray.

All Christians work to be in intimate relationships with others.

All Christians are challenged to give of themselves so to rely more on God.

All Christians have a mission of building up the kingdom.

And all Christians, like it or not, fail along the way.

As I continue to grow in my love for the Lord and faithfulness to his mission—a path that I have in many ways just begun—I have been privileged at every turn with wisdom and powerful moments of inspiration from those who have gone before me, with the lives of men and women who have made me who I am and who I am becoming. What happens after we say yes may not be the easiest, but it is my hope that this book will help it all be more fulfilling.

• • • • • •

chapter one

_____

Discernment Never Ends

"What are you going to do with your life?" For many, there is no greater anxiety-inducing question in all the world. While the answer to this question used to mean very little—merely a statement about how one made a living, a small determinant of who one was as a person—today's world knows that the answer to this question can determine everything. Social status. Self-worth. Marital and familial options. *Legacy.*

With so much pressure placed on just a few simple decisions, I have watched many high school and college friends crumble under the stress. Some work themselves into an anxious breakdown over their future; others avoid the question entirely for fear of it. A cloud seems to loom over their heads. Having just moved beyond the comfort of childhood, they immediately find themselves forced to decide the rest of their lives in an instant: What are you going to do with your life, *and when are you going to start doing it?* Decisions need to be made and they need to be made now. Don't mess this up.

I was by no means immune to such outside pressures. In fact, I felt them when I was still very young. As early as twelve years old I started thinking about which college I should attend; at fifteen, I began worrying about finding a career that would suit me; at seventeen, the thought of married family life became real. Before me were immense decisions, and even though I knew that I had some time to figure everything out, I also knew that the most important thing in life was doing just that: finding definitive and permanent answers to these questions. Once I figured out what I wanted to do with my life—and fast—everything would be easier.

You can imagine my great joy, then—and what makes my story quite different from many of my friends—when I actually *did* answer these questions for myself at a young age. At twenty-one, after a little over a year of intense discernment, I decided that I was going to spend my life in poverty, chastity, and obedience in the way of St. Francis of Assisi, a brotherhood of men centered in prayer and devoted to the life of the Church and society's poor—a decision that did not come easily or without consequence. I nonetheless found myself at the end of it at peace and assured in a way that I had never felt before. Whereas the rest of my friends spent their senior year stressed about the future, while some of them even today struggle to find what they want to do with their lives, I found myself in a place of confident celebration: I was a victor who had accomplished life's most important task. And now I could relax. Often over the following years people would tell me, "It is so amazing that you know what you want to do so young." And it was. The test, it seemed, had been finished; the question answered and put away. God, I believed at the time, had spoken to me in a clear and powerful way, calling me to this life, and I found myself where I was supposed to be. Others were trudging along, looking for their right path, and my discernment was over.

Or so I thought.

While I had no doubt taken a huge step forward in life and was blessed with a clear direction to follow, I soon came to realize that this notion of figuring out what I was going to do with my life in the grand sense was not as altogether stabilizing or permanently assuring as I was led to believe. Sure, I had made some decisions for myself that had obviously focused the possibilities of my life, but I was far from done discerning. As soon as I found myself comfortable with one decision, another question popped up. And then another. And then another. Shortly into my first year with the friars, I realized that, even if I *had* permanently decided a few years back to live my life as a Franciscan friar, I most certainly had *not* finished discerning with God what it was that I was supposed to do each and every day.

This post, written the evening of my renewal of vows during my fourth year, captures this ongoing process.

Discernment Never Ends

During the second week of July 2010, I decided that I wanted to be a Franciscan friar. Sitting in a chapel all alone that night, a flood of clarity came over me. I realized that, even though I had been struggling for months about what I should do, I had actually made the decision in my heart a long time ago. It was time to admit it to myself and stand by it: "I want to be a Franciscan friar," I said out loud. Since that moment, nothing has changed. In terms of my commitment to the life, I could have received my habit, made solemn vows, and began living the life of a friar that evening in July six years ago. I was that sure then and remain that sure today.

Is that to say that I fully knew what that commitment would mean or that I was prepared to do so? No, surely not. Nor does it mean that everything in my years as a friar has been affirming of that desire either. There have been bumps and bruises along the way, moments of disillusionment and crisis, and my understanding of what that original desire to be a friar meant has certainly been refined. Work needed to be done on my part— and continues to be done— to turn that desire into a formal, conscious, prepared commitment.

And yet, the point remains: In terms of discerning whether or not I want to stay for the rest of my life as a friar, my discernment ended more than five years ago in that chapel.

This, I would like to make very clear, is not the norm among people entering our Order. In fact, I would venture a guess to say that it is almost never the case. Guys don't come into postulancy (the first year of formation) sure of where they're supposed to be for the rest of their lives or ready to make any formal commitment. Even after two, three years of living with the friars, many guys aren't there yet.

And they don't have to be.

Becoming a solemnly professed friar is an intentionally long engagement. As I'm sure I've mentioned before, the formation process to make solemn vows in our Order takes at least five years (in my province, the minimum is six years), and no formal commitment takes place until the end of the second year. That's a lot of time—time to try on the life, ask questions, struggle with challenges, and overcome doubts and fears. Like anything else, it rarely happens overnight.

But even if it seemingly does and others find themselves in my position—sure of where I'm headed and ready to get there—discernment in the broader sense does not stop. As a Franciscan friar, I may have moved beyond the initial question of whether or not I want to be a friar in the first place, but I will never move beyond the questions of how to live this vocation out in the world today.

How am I called to live?

Who am I called to serve?

What does it mean to be a brother?

These are questions that can never be answered definitively. As the world changes, as we incorporate new brothers into the Order, as the Church presents new needs, and as I change with experience and knowledge, the way in which I and others answer these questions will inevitably change.

This evening, five members of my house will join the four others on their internship year in renewing our vows to the Franciscan Order for another year, formally recommitting ourselves to a life of poverty, chastity, and obedience in the way of St. Francis of Assisi. For some, this is a moment that has required great discernment, evaluation, and preparation to determine that this path was still the one for them; for others it is simply another step along the way towards something that we committed ourselves to a long time ago. Today, that's not really what's important though, and certainly not the focus of my reflection. The point that I see in all of this is that, no matter where we are on the journey, our discernment never stops; it only changes its form.

This is as much the case for Franciscans discerning religious life as it is for all Christians: Many of us have no question whether or not we want to remain a Christian and live out our baptismal promises, but the question of how we do it will never end. A life in Christ, no matter its form, requires that we always be discerning

His call and ready to respond in the way that our world needs us most.

While the big decisions in life—education, profession, marital and family status—are obviously important in determining a tremendous amount of what we can and cannot do, I have learned that they are not the only decisions, nor are they necessarily even the most important ones. So often we get so concerned about making the decision about our life that we forget to actually live it; we spend half of our time focused on making the decision, and then once we have made it, the other half resting on the fact that it is now complete. Discernment of God's will is not a matter of finite, ready-to-complete-and-move-on decisions, but an ongoing process of constantly requesting God's assistance each and every day.

This point was made absolutely clear to me in my novitiate, when, to the great surprise of my fellow novice classmates, one of the formators told our whole group: "You are not called to be a Franciscan friar."

For those not yet sure about what they are "going to do with their lives," in the midst of the agonizing ordeal of discerning, hearing these words may in fact come as welcome relief. Especially if they are spoken by someone who actually has the authority to deny one entry into a religious community, these words may bring much-wanted closure to a long period of discernment. For those of us on the *other* side of that agonizing ordeal, having already happily made the decision to join and now more than a year into the process of *becoming* a Franciscan friar, these words are not quite as relieving. "You are not called to be a Franciscan friar," he repeated. "None of you."

After the shock had worn off and he explained himself, we came to realize he intended it as a dramatic attention-grabbing technique and not as an order to go pack our rooms and leave immediately. That was comforting. Really, the point of the friar's statement was to remind us that our essential call from God was simple and general: "All that God calls us to be is a disciple of Jesus Christ. Nothing more."

Too often, I think, we promote this idea that God has a hyper-specific plan for our lives and that the point of discernment is to find that singular, correct path God has laid out for us among the infinite number of incorrect ones. There is but *one* path, *one* "soul mate," *one* vocation, *one* way of living to please God...and our role in life is simply to figure it out and choose it above the other, lesser options God doesn't want for us. As a result, we work ourselves into anxious fits over every decision, big or small, not because we are concerned primarily with serving God as best we can, but because we are fearful that we may choose the *wrong* one and so be stuck with an inferior life. What is often framed as a God-centered process, the act of determining the will of God, too often turns out to be a very *self*-centered one: Our concern is finding the perfect path *for us*.

Naturally, this is not what discernment is all about, and when we think about it this way we know that our premise is completely wrong. Quite obviously, there are any number of ways to please God, and in making big life decisions there are always *multiple* good options from which to choose. While certain options may fit with our personality, lifestyle, hopes, dreams, and needs of the Church better than others— and God, no doubt, cares about those things as they relate to us—we can never forget that those things are inconsequential details in the mind of God. In the *ultimate* sense, all that God wills for us is that we be disciples of Jesus Christ. Is there only one way to do that? What I've found, recorded here in one of my favorite, most emotionally challenging reflections, is that faithfully following God can lead even similar people in different directions.

A Life Worth Living

On Saturday, July 4, 2015, Father Dhiya Aziz, OFM, an Iraqi Franciscan friar serving as a missionary in Syria, was taken by an "unknown armed brigade" for a supposed brief interview with the local Emir. He never returned and no one has heard from his since.

Fr. Dhiya is not alone, in Syria or in history. He is not the first priest to go missing in Syria this year, and he is certainly not the first priest to go missing in violent areas of the world. As representatives of a worldwide Christian organization and being sources of resistance to injustice and violence, priests have often been prime targets for militant groups in the past. (One has only to look to El Salvador in the 1980s for more than a handful of examples.)

So, what are religious doing in such places walking around with bull's-eyes on their backs? This was the topic of discussion at dinner last night: "Pretty soon someone is going to have to act on this. It doesn't look like it's getting any better.... Michael [minister general of the OFMs] should tell these guys to get out of there." Point taken. When a situation has gotten so bad that nearly four million people have fled the country since January 2012 and the city in which one is ministering, Yacoubieh, was completely abducted by the militant Islamic regime two years ago, one could certainly deem volunteering to transfer to this place, as Fr. Dhiya did, to be useless, futile, or even reckless. Wouldn't it be better, at that point, to flee as well, saving oneself for another day of ministry rather than almost guaranteeing one's fate as a martyr? Are we called to be martyrs or called to realize that we have been given a life worth living, not throwing away?

What comes to mind for me in situations like these are a handful of well-made movies based on true stories *(Of Gods and Men, The Mission, Romero)*. The most prominent in this situation for me is **Beyond the Gates**, the (mostly) true, very Catholic story of a priest and teacher caught in the Rwandan genocide. Obviously against the genocide of their people, they turn the school into a refugee camp and receive aid from the United Nations. Eventually, though, the UN determines that they can no longer stay and offers the two men an out: Being foreigners, they can safely transport them across the border, leaving the Tutsis behind, no doubt to be killed as soon as they leave.

For most of the movie, the two men struggle with this question, ultimately deciding on opposite fates: The priest decides to stay and is eventually killed; the teacher decides to leave and safely returns home.

For me, both of them made the correct decision. The priest, knowing with all of his heart that this is where he was supposed to be, could not imagine being anywhere other than right where his people were suffering:

"You asked me, Joe, where is God in everything that is happening here, in all the suffering? I know exactly where he is. He's right here. With these people. Suffering. His love is here. More intense and profound than I have ever felt. And my heart is here, Joe. My soul. And if I leave I think I may not find it again."

For him, it was not about preserving his life for another day, it was about living it today. He had found God. What could he want with safety or comfort?

The teacher, seeing the bigger picture, saw the reality of the situation: Whether he stayed or left, everyone was going to die. He could not change that with all of his might. Instead, God had given him a gift: Because of his white skin and European nationality, he was given preferential treatment by the UN and offered a way out. He could live another day, fight another fight, and make something productive out of his situation. It wasn't fair, but it was what he believed to be the best option in a bad situation.

In the end, his decision was not without consequences and the priest's was not without positive effect. It is here that I return to the situation we face today in Syria, among other places. For the people remaining in these situations, whether it be Rwanda in 1994 or Syria in 2015, the poorest and weakest do not have the opportunity to flee, only the opportunity to see everything they know and love leave them one by one. While the teacher had considered the fact that his friends would all eventually die, he did not realize until the moment his truck was driving away how much pain his decision would inflict on them while they remained alive: "Joe...where are you going?" one friend called with despair. "You promised!" While he left for his safety, she remained, left to contemplate not only her imminent death, but the fact that someone she considered her brother abandoned her to face that death alone. The priest may not have accomplished anything to prolong her life, but his presence until the end served as witness that it was a life worth living.

Putting myself in this situation, thinking about myself in Rwanda or Syria, I can honestly say that I have no idea what I would do. Just writing this post has evoked so much emotion in me that I have had to take a few breaks just to finish. Add in personal relationships with people suffering without any hope for safety and a healthy dose of fear, and it's likely that I would crawl into a state of physical and emotional paralysis, unable to actually make a decision at all. I don't know. What I do know, though, is that I admire anyone willing to stand with those left behind, to truly be who we say we are as Franciscans, the least among society.

I hope that you will join me in praying for our brother Dhiya Aziz for his safe return, for all the people of Syria and countries around the world where people are left to suffer, and for each of us, that we may find the courage to stand with the lowest and least around us, not because we can necessary change their situation but because we can show them that their lives are worth living.

With a life in Jesus as our foundation and nothing else, God's call to us and our ultimate purpose in life tend to look very different. Thinking less about the decisions themselves and more about the life those decisions effect, we realize that what matters most to God is ultimately not *what* we choose but the amount of love that those decisions create in our lives; where we go to school, what we do for a living, and our familial life matters to God only to the extent that what we choose enables us to live as Christ-like as we can. All that God wills and all that God calls us to be is his adopted sons and daughters. That's it. As much as my fellow brothers and I were blessed to have answered what we believed to be the important discernment question of our day—what are you going to do with your life—what we realized was that the answer to that question was simply the means to answering the *truly* important question of life: "Lord, what do I need to do today to be a better disciple of yours?" Both of the men in Rwanda had clear paths set in their lives; they had answered the big questions for themselves. But the fact that one was a priest and another a teacher did not matter in the slightest. What mattered was that they acted in that moment as disciples of Jesus Christ. Their lives were defined, not by the ultimate decision, but by the individual ones they chose to make each day. "Lord, what do I need to do today to be a better disciple of yours?"

For some, this simplest of questions offers instant clarity and direction by stripping away all but what is essential to Christian life. When St. Francis heard the Gospel read of Jesus sending out the disciples two-by-two to preach, he knew immediately this was what he was supposed to do, exclaiming, "That is what I want!" For others—maybe most people—it only complicates the issue further. *With so many amazing ways to live as a disciple of Christ, how could I ever know for sure what God wants from* me? No doubt, discerning the mind of God is a formidable task, one not to be treated lightly and usually not with certainty. But it is a task that we can and must do as Christians. Throughout Scripture, God speaks to his people in ways that they can understand; in the lives of ordinary people, God continues to make his presence known.

So why so much difficulty with our simple question? The problem, as I see it, is not that we fail to ask God for guidance in our prayer, nor is it that God chooses not to answer us. No, the problem is that *we do not know where to look for the answer.* Sure, we prayerfully ask God for help, we expect and so listen for a response, but we wouldn't know what a response was if it came up and bit us on the nose! So often I speak with people who say they pray to God and ask for a response but don't feel like they ever get one. When I ask them what a response would look like—in other words, how would they know that it was God speaking to them—they have no idea. No wonder discernment can be so agonizing to some people: It is like talking into a phone and then looking around the room for a response. Even if the person on the other end of the line is shouting perfectly clear answers we will never hear it because we are too busy contemplating the kitchen table or microwave to notice! Knowing what to even reflect on is most of the battle.

So where do we look? Often, the easiest place to start is with our own feelings. In this post from 2011, a time when I was discerning whether or not I was called to be ordained to the priesthood, my focus was on what I wanted to do.

Discerning the Priesthood: Part One

When I started to discern religious life, there were two questions I had to answer: 1) Am I called to be a Franciscan? and 2) Am I called to be a priest? (Without wasting a lot of time on the technical side, I do want to make it clear that not all Franciscans are priests, and that all Franciscans are supposed to be viewed as equal brothers whether they are ordained or not.) Clearly, I have answered question number one with a loud and clear yes. When it comes to question number two, there are still some big questions I have that leave me hesitant and still searching for an answer.

Though it would seem like an oversimplification of the matter, an interesting question that I have been advised to ponder is this: "Do you like doing things that priests do?" The only way that this question can be answered is by imagining oneself in that position, and wondering how it would feel. Every time I'm at Mass, confession, or any of the other sacraments, I ask myself that question: "Can I imagine myself doing that, and would I like it?"

In a typical on-the-fence response, I have to say that I would and I wouldn't. I love the Eucharist and find it to be the most beautiful Christian experience possible, but I'm not sure if I want to be the one doing it. I have no problem speaking in front of people, and I have enjoyed my roles as altar server and such, but there is a big difference between setting the table and actually breaking the bread.

Hearing confession, on the other hand, is something in which I would find great joy as a priest. I've often found myself in many counseling or mediating roles over the years and cherish deeply the conversations I've had with those willing to open up and trust me in such a way. I can think of few greater things than aiding others in their journey from separation to communion and find it to be a wonderful privilege of being a stand-in for Christ.

Although it may seem superficial at first, an excellent place I always like to start is with my own feelings. *Does this bring me joy?* While contemplating one's desires may simply reveal personal preference and may only reflect selfish ambitions rather than shedding light on God's selfless will, framing the question in this way may reveal more than we might think. What we are asking is not what makes us "happy," a fleeting and superficial emotion, nor are we asking what makes us "comfortable," a stagnant situation that often leads to apathy; we are asking to find what brings such a sense of purpose and belonging deep within us that we *rejoice* at the greatness we have found. Joy is something that gives us life. It is something that gets us out of bed in the morning. It is a lasting sense of positive meaning, something that not only survives the hard times but carries us through them.

If that is the way we feel about something—or maybe more importantly, if we do *not* feel this way about something—we cannot ignore it in our discernment. God, I truly believe, does not call us to a life of misery and despair. And how could he? If what we are seeking is to live as a disciple of Jesus Christ, a life in which we seek to be in perfect union with the source of joy itself, the presence or absence of joy in our lives is a tremendous indication of how close we are to our right calling.

When people ask me how I knew that I wanted to be a friar, this is exactly what I tell them. Even when I am angry with my brothers, even when I am disappointed in myself, even when I struggle to reconcile my own experience with that of the Church, I find a sense of peace and joy waking up every morning in the friary. I may not necessarily be happy. I am usually not comfortable. But I find myself rejoicing in the life that I get to live. For me, that feeling can only come from God.

Of course, this feeling is not the only one that can come from God, and lest our whole discernment be through the lens of our own personal feelings and desires, I have to admit that I did not *find* my vocation by searching my feelings. No, no, no. Even in the post above, you can see that following my own feelings could get me only so far. While it is certainly how I know *now* that I am in the right place, the very fact that I considered religious life in the first place had very little to do with my own will or desire! I was quite comfortable with my old life and wonderful girlfriend—thank you very much—and had it been simply up to my own desires, I probably would not have changed a thing. No, when discerning *God's* will, our own feelings can be a good guide, but they always have to be taken with another question: What does the world—specifically God's Church— need that I can provide?

A question for which I certainly have a few concrete suggestions of my own, I would like to hold off on any specific ideas until the fifth chapter of this book and instead focus now on the process itself, leaning on the final phrase "that I can provide." For this, once again, I have found the easiest way to discern God's will is to ask a simple question: What am I good at?

Like our discernment of feelings, a personal inventory of gifts and skills can be nothing more than a selfish reflection of how amazing we believe ourselves to be, but it can also be much more. If we truly believe that God is the giver of all gifts, that everything we have and everything we are able to do is from God, then an honest and sober look at ourselves can reveal a bit of God's will in us. Like the parable of the talents, God does not want us to bury our treasure for fear that we might lose it; we are called to multiply it for the sake of the world and God's kingdom. Why else would we have been given such a gift? For some, these gifts are obvious. Use them for God's people!

But that, in a sense, is not even at the heart of what I am suggesting. For some, nothing immediate comes to mind and we may not believe that we are capable of anything extraordinary. *What could God use* me *for? Surely, there is someone better.* If this sounds like you, join the illustrious club of prophets and servants throughout salvation history through whom God has performed incredible miracles! Whether it was Moses and his lack of eloquence, Jonah and his fear, Peter and his "rock" headedness, or Thomas and his doubt, the true heart of this question is not about determining what we are capable of, on our own and based on what society values—it is determining what God is capable of through us that will give God glory. When I ask, then, "what am I good at?" I am not primarily asking about possible award-winning talents that I possess, but rather, what about me is capable, with the grace of God, of bearing fruit in the community for the sake of the kingdom? Put another way, in what ways does the community compliment me and ask for my help? When discerning in this sense, we are not concerned with what we may be best at or worthy of celebrity status. All that matters is our ability to make God present in a new way. As much as a reflection on what we *want* to do is important, truly understanding what God's community *needs from us* can direct us to where God wants us most.

This is where discernment gets fun and not so fun. Much more than following our feelings alone, being willing to use what God has given us for the sake of the world may mean doing what we initially do not want to do and being stretched far beyond our comfort zones. All of a sudden, we find ourselves like Moses, unprepared and overwhelmed, outside of what we normally do and plan for ourselves, wondering if serving God is really for us. The further we go in discernment and the more we open ourselves up to God's will and not our own, we may find ourselves less willing to say yes as strongly as we did before. *Lord, I want to follow you, but please not in that way!* It is here, in this second level of discerning God's will, that I found myself with one of the most important reflections of my life.

Yes, But Under My Conditions

As I continue to discern whether God is calling me to be ordained or not, I have come up with an analogy that describes my current disposition: I am like a potential parent that says, "I want to have a child...but only if it's a boy."

Like the would-be parent who is comfortable with the possibility of having a catch with his son or teaching him how to ride a bike, I have taken the big step forward over the past two years in acknowledging that there are some aspects of "being a father" that are appealing enough to me to take on the new role.

The problem with this sentiment is that it is not open to all of the possibilities one may face. What if it's a girl? Mentally handicapped? Doesn't like baseball? Like the parent, there are aspects of ordination I am unwilling to accept at this point in my formation. What if I were assigned to an upper-middle class suburban parish so removed from poverty and hardship that it became difficult not to fall into complacency? Or, what if I were made pastor of a one-priest church, required to take on large amounts of administrative duties and left tied down to one particular schedule and place? These are among the many hypothetical situations (along with a few theological issues that I won't mention here) that leave me saying, "Yes, but under my conditions."

Like a potential parent, I don't think this is the proper disposition one can have to take on such a role. To be ordained is to say yes without condition, open and prepared for anything the kingdom of God needs here on earth. It means being a malleable instrument God can use whenever and however he pleases.

To do so with conditions would be to misunderstand the role entirely; "yes, but under my conditions" is not really a yes at all.

True discipleship, as I have experienced it in Scripture and in the life of the saints, is being able to say yes without reservations. When Jesus called his original followers, the Gospels say that they "left everything and followed Him." When St. Francis heard the cross speak to him and tell him to "rebuild my Church," he immediately went out and did so. As the cliché goes, there were no "ifs, ands, or buts" in their responses, no reservations or personal motivations that held them back. There was simply a willingness to go when Jesus called. *That* is what we are called to discern and strive for—a life free of barriers in saying yes to Jesus.

Among the largest barriers I have had to break down in my life was the possibility of joining religious life. A faithful and active Catholic all my life, I knew when I was in high school that I wanted to do all I could for God. Whatever God needed for God's Church, I would do it. I went to church more often. Tried to be nicer to people I didn't like. Donated my money to the poor. I even went to a university that would prepare me for a lifetime of ministry. And yet, I soon realized that I had drawn lines in the sand of what I would and would not do. While I told interested adults when I was young, "Yes, I am open to a vocation to the priesthood," and, "I feel called to married life, but am willing to do whatever God wants," I always knew that there was absolutely no truth to that. The fact of the matter is that I had never seriously considered it for a second. My saying that I was called to married life—a perfectly good vocation that I'm sure I could have lived just fine—was not so much the result of actual prayer and discernment as it was an easy way to avoid the question. I was afraid of what God might want from me and so I just chose not to ask. I put up a barrier to discipleship, a limit on how far my yes would take me and how willing I was to serve God.

Is this to say that unless we all join religious communities, take vows of poverty, chastity, and obedience, and live ascetic lives that we are not truly living a life of discipleship? Of course not! If everyone lived this life, there would be no faithful disciples raising children, working in society, and doing all the other things necessary for building up the kingdom. It is to say that each and every one of us needs to be *open* to that call—and to the call of marriage—and to the call of being a prophet—a martyr—a mother or father—a leader— and anything else that the kingdom of God needs. Being a disciple does not mean that we are *called* to do anything and everything. It means we are open to serving God in any way without counting the cost. "Let your yes mean yes," Jesus tells us, and not, as I find so often in my life, "Yes, but under my conditions."

Likely, this will sound more than a bit overwhelming to most. When we think about our lives, it is very easy to see that none of us lives with the freedom we see in the saints and idealize in Scripture. To some extent, we are all struggling with our own limitations, our own failings of being a perfect disciple. And that is okay. As I have found in my life, conversion does not take place overnight. Progress in this life does not appear from one day to the next but is the result of many years of daily working to follow Jesus better each and every day. I wrote about this after having been a friar for three years.

Learning to Live Radically

I remember quite clearly how overwhelmed I felt the first summer I ever had a homework assignment. (To this day, it still seems unjust!) It was before my junior year of high school and the teacher wanted us to read *The Scarlet Letter* and write a two-page essay on the book. I was beside myself. After reading two chapters, I begged my dad to let me switch into the easier section. "I can't do it!" He denied my request. I wrote the paper, got a B in the course, and ended up learning just about everything I know about writing that year. I hate it when dads are right.

When I look back on that time, it makes me laugh a bit because I would kill to have such an easy assignment. This semester, I have four different classes that require a two-page paper every week, and seem to be handling it "okay"! Who I am today and what I am capable of is far beyond what was the case when I was sixteen. The same has been true at every stage of my life: At each new level, I started off overwhelmed with all that I couldn't do, only to find that, with time and training, I was able to do it.

The reason I tell this story is not to show how great of a learner I am or even to spout the cliché that "you can do anything you set your mind to!" No. (I thought that calculus was overwhelming when I started it, and I will forever believe that it is overwhelming. Growth doesn't always happen.) What I am trying to say is that we are often more capable of growth than we realize, and more importantly, that conversion often takes a long time.

I look to my life as a Christian and a Franciscan friar as another example. Today, I live a fairly ascetic life compared to what I did in college. I have less freedom, less time, spend less money, and own fewer things. I pray at least three times per day. I have more than one time looked at my life and decided to do something much more inconveniently or uncomfortably in order to be more energy conscious. If college me would have looked at the way I live now, with all of the many things I have picked up over the years as a way to live out my call to discipleship, I would have been absolutely overwhelmed. I can't do it!

Do you know what? Four years ago, that was true. There is no way that I could have taken on four years worth of conversions at one time, redefining every aspect of my life all at once. And yet, here we are. I am living this way and I am loving it. I am a person today who is no longer overwhelmed with the same demands of Christian discipleship as I was yesterday. Conversion has taken place, and in some cases, it took four years (some things will probably take much longer!)

So what does this have to do with anything? Very simply, small conversions amount to big ones over time. We may look at someone like St. Francis of Assisi or Mother Teresa and say, "There is no way that I could ever be that holy, that devoted to Christ." And you're right: Right now, you can't. But just remember, at one time, St. Francis was just Giovanni "Francesco" Bernardone, an arrogant kid in nice clothes who wanted the glory of being a knight; at one time; Mother Teresa was just Anjezë Gonxhe Bojaxhiu, a little Albanian girl admiring the lives of missionaries. They weren't always saints. Over a lifetime they learned to live radically for the Gospel, one step at a time, until they had become a completely changed person from when they started.

The same can absolutely be true for us. We are all called to be saints. Really. Do you think that you could be a saint? Probably not if you focus on just the finished product. As a sixteen-year-old, I couldn't even see myself writing one two-page paper over the entire summer, let alone four per week. And yet, here we are. Jesus doesn't ask of us perfect discipleship all at once, but he does ask that we face what challenges us today with a step forward. It may not be a big step, but small steps over a lifetime makes for quite a journey. May we, like the saints, use every moment we're given to learn to live each moment more radically than the last.

In one sense, what I love about this reflection is that it forces us to stay present to the moment, to forget the ultimate questions of "what are you going to do with your life" and focus exclusively on what we are capable of doing in this moment. Because, really, what is the point of worrying about things we cannot do or placing impossible expectations on ourselves? My goal in life is not some far-off accomplishment, some idealized sense of self in the future; while true some day, they are but dreams to us now that only serve to overwhelm us. My goal, rather, is to answer our chief question: "Lord, what do I need to do today to be a better disciple of yours?" Such a question can only be answered in the here and now, with the broken and incomplete self that I am. I may not be my finished product coming into glory just yet, but I can answer that question today. In doing so, ironically enough, we find ourselves reaching those very things we are unable to conceive today.

But there is another reason I love this reflection, and it is somewhat the opposite of the first: It focuses us backwards to the past. Although discernment is often the process of looking to the future with the hope of a greater union with God, we are also able to look back and see with clearer eyes the many ways we are *already within it*. It is often said that "hindsight is 20/20" when making decisions, and I think it is just as true with discerning our life in Christ. For as difficult as it is to see progress in our lives in the present or to determine where

God is in our lives right now, the past is often an open book. When I look at where I have been and what it took to get me where I am, what emerges is a clear path that seems not to be possible by any other course, a path with growth and understanding, a path that seems to have been guided by one stronger than I. In prayerfully reviewing the past and not just analyzing it, noticing patterns and repeated situations along the way, I cannot help but see that, even though progress is not always constant or direct, I am a different person than I was before, and God has so clearly been the one shaping me along the way.

Lectio Divina of Life

It was after a wonderful conversation about the ancient practice of lectio divina, the prayerful repeated reading of a scriptural text, that my spiritual director made the connection that the process we follow there is the same process we follow in our own lives. What he meant by this was that the journey of our life is something that can be prayerfully entered into, rather than just analyzed, and that we can experience God in reliving, or rereading, our life's journey. In some ways, the stories of our past are unchanging, set in stone. But as we read our life's stories and allow time for meditation, prayer, and contemplation, we are called to a deeper understanding of what each event means to us.

The clear example I have right now is my novitiate. I believe very strongly that the majority of the stuff that "happened" to me during novitiate, the bulk of what we may call "revelation," occurred in the first three months. The remaining nine months I believe I spent trying to understand and integrate what I had experienced into myself.

What I also realized was that life is a cyclical set of situations that recur on a regular basis; progress, then, looks much more like a spiral staircase than it does a ladder. We want to think sometimes that we can find a solution to our problems that will leave them in our past, stepping up a step on the ladder never to come back down. And yet, a short period of time later, we find ourselves face-to-face with the same problem. Have we regressed? Not necessarily. Just like in *lectio divina* and just like walking up a spiral staircase, each step brings us somewhere new and yet ever closer to where we first began. While I found myself becoming frustrated with the lack of "progress" in my life, I realized that with true introspection, by recognizing the situation, meditating on it, bringing it to prayer, and then contemplating with God, there was something new that I could bring to the situation. I may have been standing in the same spot as before, but my perspective had changed; one floor higher, there was a slightly new vantage point on the same situation from which to act. Once I chose how to act, there began a new cycle of prayerfully reading that situation into the corpus of my life.

I remember gathering one night in college with a few of my Catholic friends to share with one another our journey of faith. For the first time in my life, I recounted aloud all of the important moments of my life, the moments that shaped me and touched me, the times that I felt God most clearly around me. It was both powerfully inspiring and cathartic at the same time, a moment of intense memory all thrown together for the first time. And something interesting happened. While I thought that I was there to share my life with the others, it was a friend of mine that spoke afterwards with great insight. Having listened to the whole story, she noticed a pattern. "Do you know that all of your stories are related to one another?" I had not. But she was right. In each of my most important stories, the times in which I related most to God and God related most to me, I found a common theme and a common call to respond. Over and over again there seemed to be the same situation calling to me. There in my past, there in the moments lost forever to history, was God speaking to me, revealing what was important to him and thus what he wanted from me.

There again, in yet another varied way, I have found that God is able to speak to those who are willing to listen. Understanding our feelings. Identifying our personal gifts. The lives of the prophets and saints. Looking to the future. Contemplating the past. In as many ways as we could possibly understand, God is calling his people to a life of discipleship, walking beside us as we discern how to act.

And yet, we know that a life of discipleship is not an easy one nor does it follow a straight path. As much as God may speak to us and help us along the way, we know that we will be faced with decisions that we simply cannot answer, questions that shake us to the bone and leave us unsure of what to do. Even as we pray, live upright lives, and call on the Lord for help, we will inevitably find ourselves in this life discerning particular situations to no end. *What should I do Lord?* It would seem, sometimes, that there is no right answer, no perfectly correct path to follow, no ultimate answer to what we are "going to do with our lives."

But no matter what we do or don't do, no matter if we get it "right" or "wrong," no matter if we figure out what we're "going to do with our lives" or take every moment in stride,

God will be there at our side guiding our path. Our goal in discernment is not to answer all of the big questions once and for all, to check boxes off a list and cast them—and God—aside until we have another question; our goal is to journey with God, to be constantly listening for the call that he has for us, the call to be a disciple of his Son in today's world. Our goal, above all else, is to live in the moment with God.

• • • • • •

chapter **two**

Living in the Moment

As an outsider looking in, it was difficult for me to get the full picture of what it meant to be a Franciscan friar. Seeing the brothers from afar and only in their public lives, all I ever saw was their work. They worked, and they worked *hard*. With gratitude in their hearts and humble service as their goal, I was inspired by this group of men who made it their life's goal to make the world a better place, going with joy and vigor to those whom society had cast out or forgotten. They were people out to change the world.

You can imagine my surprise then, in my first meeting as a postulant with the friars, when the formation director told our class that Franciscans were first and foremost men of prayer. "Unless prayer is the foundation for everything you do and the most important thing in your lives," we were told, "you will not become good Franciscans." Prayer? Really? I knew, of course, that prayer was important to our lives, but I didn't join this life to pray! If that is what I wanted, I thought, I would have joined a monastery and become a monk. No, I joined the friars to do stuff, to build up the kingdom of God! But the friar continued: "You are going to have to put off 'saving the world' for at least a year. It will still be there. This year is about laying the foundation of prayer that you will need for the rest of your lives as friars."

A look at the year's schedule showed he was not kidding. Spending only three days a week in active ministry, our time would be almost entirely filled with internally focused activities: workshops, classes on Franciscan history and life, days of recollection, and yes, *two* week-long silent retreats! For eight days at a monastery and five days at a hermitage, we were not only expected to pray, we were expected to be *silent* while doing it, and—if you can believe it—to disconnect completely from our phones, computers, and music players for the entire time.

Gasp!

As a twenty-two-year-old at the time, a child of the technological age, I am not sure if I can truly capture the shock that such an experience can have without coming off too dramatically or overly flippant, but these were game changers for me. While I was not a foreigner to retreats as they are experienced in high school and college—that is, weekends that are a mix of prayer, community building, and relaxed fun—I realized something very unsettling about myself no more than ten minutes into the first silent retreat with the friars: I had never *truly* been silent before in my life. Like so many of this age, my world was one of constant stimulation, always just a click away from entertainment, knowledge, social interaction, or anything else I wanted. Even in prayer, there was always an activity, always someone else around, always something to keep my attention...to keep me from being truly silent.

What would happen if I shut everything off, cleared my

schedule, and completely opened my heart and mind to God? Like it or not, I would soon find out. As I shared after my eight-day retreat with the monks, it was, ironically, when I gave up even trying to pray properly, when I stopped trying to "focus," when I stopped trying to *do something*, that my prayer life came alive.

Living in the Moment

I'm not sure if everyone else is like this, but I have a very active imagination. I find myself with my head in the clouds quite often, either remembering some past experience or creating an elaborate hypothetical situation in the future, oftentimes taking both sides of an argument or practicing eloquent dissertations. I've been told that this doesn't make me crazy (really!), and that it can actually be a great form of prayer. On the other hand, it can be an escape that leaves me having never experienced the present moment; to only contemplate the past and future leaves no room for experiencing a great homily, the beauty of nature, the particularities of the Mass, or most tragically, an experience of direct communication with God. My goal for this retreat was to fight the temptation to drift off and to stay focused on the present, to live in the moment.

And so we began. *Ora et labora.* Pray and work. St. Benedict's great motto was our Rule for a week. Off went the cell phone, and quiet went the mouth for the majority of the day.

Each day was greatly dictated by the schedule for prayer: Seven times a day, we dropped whatever we were doing and met the monks for a highly formalized prayer. This included Vigils (4:45 am), Lauds (7:00 am), Mass (9:00 am), Sext (12:00 pm), None (3:00 pm), Vespers (6:30 pm), and Compline (8:15 pm). Though I found some of the hours to be a bit monotonous, at least intellectually I found the commitment to prayer to be quite profound. Even for minor hours, such as Sext and None that lasted literally six minutes, no one ever missed it. Because prayer is the most important part of their life, other tasks had to work their way around the prayer schedule. This was a great witness to the rest of the world that prays as an afterthought or only in its "free time."

Between prayers, we were free to read, go for walks, journal, pray privately, or best of all, nap extensively. With nothing required for us to do and being banned from our phones and unnecessary conversation, I saw the week as an excellent time to relax while being productive enough to catch up on some reading and writing.

To my great surprise, however, there can actually be such a thing as too much free time! And because it is very easy to forget to focus on the present and revert to a normal task-oriented way of thinking, I became restless within just a few days when there wasn't enough to occupy my time. Without the news, music, conversation, tasks, games, or television to keep my attention, I was left in a world of which I was unfamiliar: silence. I even found myself treating prayer as something to be completed, allotting specific amounts of time for it and expecting certain results. In doing so, I inadvertently focused my attention more on how much time I had left and what my next task was than on my experience at that moment.

In the afternoon of day four, I hit a wall. I had no interest in reading. I had just taken a nap. I had nothing to journal about. The thought of formal prayer didn't entice me. I was in a state of lethargy that left me feeling apathetic, and honestly, a bit helpless. What was I going to do for another seven hours before bed and for four more days?

Forcing myself to get up, I walked over to the chapel and sat down with one goal: Just exist. I told myself not to worry about how long I was going to be there, what I was going to focus on, how I was supposed to pray. Just exist. Just live in the moment. Instead of closing my eyes and trying to block out the sounds around me, I embraced every one of my senses as a way to take part in the present moment. I thought to myself, "Since Jesus in his Eucharistic presence is in this specific place, I will just sit here and experience the surroundings with him."

What was I hoping to get out of it? Nothing but a shared experience with a friend.

When was I going to finish? Whenever I didn't want to enjoy the moment any more.

That was it. Just exist, together.

Though it was my goal from the start, it took time for me to actually realize what that meant. When I finally did, it was amazing how freeing of an experience it was to just sit and enjoy the moment with him. In that moment, for however long it lasted, I was given a faith that hadn't been there before, connected in a way unlike any other in the past. It was unexpected. It was life giving. It shaped the rest of the week.

And yet, it was only the first wall I had to break through. No sooner did I have this revelation did I fall into the comfort of complacency: Now that I've had such a great experience, I'm good for a while. It was as if it gave me a free pass to stop seeking, to stop wanting more experiences, to be comfortable in the current state. Had the retreat lasted only three days, I would have never gotten to the point of desperation that forced me to let myself go; had it lasted only six days, I would have never had to deal with the complacency that followed.

At the start of any relationship, there is always the anxious sense that you need to be doing or saying something to prevent any awkward silences. Nothing is more uncomfortable than that silence! Everything is formal, and you are always worrying if the other person is bored or if you should be *doing* something. It is an exhausting and stressful time. Until, one day, something changes. All of a sudden, you realize that simply *being* with the other person is good enough; there is no need for anything more than the presence of the other person. *Oh how I used to love sitting with my girlfriend on the couch doing nothing! How I still love to be with my close friends, just hanging out.* No longer any pretense or stress, no longer a need to impress or entertain the other, you reach a point when you are so comfortable together—and so happy with that comfort—that what matters most is not *what* you are doing, it is *who* you are doing it with.

Sitting alone in the crypt church that afternoon, I experienced that feeling with Jesus for the very first time. Praying there, hoping that something would "happen" or I would receive some revelation, I remember being tremendously annoyed at first by a restless monk disturbing my prayer. Time and again he walked through the chapel noisily looking for something. Marching up and down the stairs, he stomped his feet slowly and heavily. Repeatedly, he slammed the door at the top of the stairs. There I was, trying to block out everything I could so I could actively listen to whatever Jesus was saying—working as hard as I could to be *doing* something so as to avoid the awkward silence—but this monk was ruining everything. I kept losing focus and thought my prayer was a waste of time. Until a simple thought came to my mind: If

Jesus is truly in this place with me, I bet he is annoyed with that monk too. *Click.* Just like that, my whole perspective on my time changed. The very thought that Jesus was there with me experiencing what I was experiencing transformed the monk from something *preventing* a focused prayer to the very thing Jesus and I were *sharing together.* At that moment, I realized that prayer was not always about doing something productive to avoid the awkward silence; sometimes, it was simply about enjoying time spent with one another doing nothing.

So often in high school and college, friends of mine would talk about their prayer lives with such excitement. They shared how Jesus was like a brother to them, maybe a close friend, or a wise guide. They spoke about the intimacy of their relationship, that they had a "personal relationship" with God that got them through life. I could never say any of that with much sincerity. Don't get me wrong! I "loved" Jesus and all he did and stood for. I was so inspired by his life that I wanted to live for the sake of his Church and even devote myself to living as a consecrated religious. But he was never *personal* to me. As I described it once to a friend, Jesus was like an amazing celebrity, maybe a friend of a friend: I had heard so much about him, was inspired by his life and work, and could not wait to meet him...someday.

That day turned out to be the fourth day of my monastery retreat in the crypt church.

And it did not stop there. I had started something very exciting. No longer a hopeless millennial fearing the silent disconnect of a personal retreat, I looked forward to my next opportunity to enter that mysterious place within me and be with the God I was beginning to know. What would I find the next time? This was the breakthrough in prayer that I had been waiting for, the catalyst I needed to build my relationship with God and truly be a "man of prayer." I was well on my way, and it felt great.

Until reality set in.

My prayer life at this point could be likened to a New Year's resolution to join a gym and get in shape. At the beginning, there is a lot of enthusiasm. The first workout is amazing. We are inspired, full of energy, and looking forward to the beach body we are about to have. The second week comes and we are still enthusiastic, but the first week was harder than we thought and now we are a little stiff and not as full of energy. A little while later, the initial enthusiasm begins to fade, the results we thought we would see sooner do not appear, and we begin to slip. At first, we skip a workout, "because I worked out really hard yesterday and need to rest my body"; then it is, "I am just a little too busy today, but I will definitely go tomorrow"; until one day we catch a glimpse at our running shoes in the closet and realize that it has been three weeks since we last went to the gym and have no interest at all in starting up again.

As foundational as my initial prayer experience was, it was not enough to make me a "man of prayer" overnight. Even on that *same retreat* I shared how quickly I had become complacent! The fact of the matter is that prayer is difficult. It is an act that defies rationality, reveals little-to-no measurable effect in our lives, and because of its inherently personal nature, is difficult to have much accountability. *Who is really going to know the quality of my prayer? Who is really going to know if I do not pray at all?* Like so many—and on more than one occasion throughout my life—I followed up a transformative experience of prayer with a lackluster response.

Something needed to change. At first motivated simply by my own disappointment in myself and knowing that my formator was right—I would not become a good friar without a good prayer life—I changed my mindset by the second year. As I described in this post after the year had ended, I decided to focus on the one thing that I could control: showing up.

My Prayer of Fidelity

Woody Allen is famously quoted as saying, "Eighty percent of life is showing up." For many, this is an example of one of those cheesy motivational quotes found on posters of soaring eagles or sunsets over mountains, feel-good lines that don't stand up to actual reason. For many, glorifying the act of showing up is akin to awarding "participation ribbons" to every kid in Little League, downplaying what really matters—skill and hard work—ultimately lowering our expectations and standards so that we're all winners. Showing up, for many, is worth very little.

It may surprise many of you then to hear that I find this line is a perfect one to describe my experience of prayer life since the beginning of novitiate. Prayer, as I have found it, is an act of fidelity.

Even for someone who has been a Christian all my life, believed in God, and found prayer to be an important practice, I have often struggled to find prayer to be a consistently fulfilling experience. Sometimes, I would finish empowered, overjoyed, and enlightened about God, myself, and the world; other times, I would leave having spent twenty minutes thinking about what I was going to do next, or worse yet, focused entirely on the question, "What the heck am I doing wasting my time with this?"

Because of this, prayer time was never among my highest priorities, and my commitment to it was sporadic at best. This was the case even up through my postulant year into novitiate. I intellectually knew that prayer was a good thing to do, but for one reason or another (too busy, bored, tired, distracted, etc.) I could still go days without intentional time for prayer.

This all changed during novitiate. While I knew that I could not control how tired, distracted, interested, comfortable, or happy I was going to be during prayer, nor could I affect the outcome of the experience, I knew that I could control my attendance. Within the first couple weeks of novitiate, I made a commitment to quietly sit in the chapel for thirty minutes a day. All I had to do was show up. And let me tell you: A lot of mornings, that's all I did. There were days that getting out of bed to sit in a cold chapel was the last thing I wanted to do. There were days when I could have spent that time doing "more important" things. There were days when I was angry at God, my brothers, or myself, and didn't want to deal with them. There were days when showing up, literally, was all I could have done. And yet, in the past I wouldn't have even done that.

What I came to realize was that showing up, having fidelity to prayer, was in fact a prayer in and of itself. I found that it offered an insight into God's fidelity to me, that God was always there, showing up for me, not because I deserved it, was particularly enjoyable to be around, or offered a fulfilling experience, but because of his commitment to my life. Showing up, even when I didn't want to, offered me the opportunity to return that love, to emulate the God who had never failed to love me.

The reason I believe I failed to experience much in my prayer life before this point, and why I continue to struggle at times, is because prayer is something that requires a lot of work, commitment, and practice. For me, eighty percent of that experience is showing up, and so that's what I do. I pray Morning and Evening Prayer each and every day, no matter how busy, and find thirty minutes a day for *lectio divina.* Do I always enjoy it? No, but I can tell you one thing: The more I show up the more I enjoy it. In the same way that one does not pick up running and immediately enjoy it or is able to run well, prayer is something that needs to be entered gradually, worked at, and persevered in.

In the end, what more is there for us to do but show up? We are always and already in the presence of God so there is nothing more we can do to call his attention; God is constantly offering us more of his grace than we can surely handle so there is no need to earn anything; and we are certainly not in control of what God may or may not be preparing us for, so there is no use in trying to assert our will over his. All we have to do and all we can ever do is show up and take part in the work of our God. Fidelity. That's my prayer.

It may sound elementary or overly simplistic, but it is one of the most important things that has ever happened to my prayer life: Just show up. Even if the only reason we show up is because of an internal sense of duty or to fulfill some obligation we have placed upon ourselves—even if prayer is nothing more than a box to be checked off in our day—checking that box off is better than not doing it. It is what we do in our other relationships, is it not? We do not always *want* to do the things we do or feel tremendous joy fulfilling our responsibilities to our friends and family. But we do them anyway. We call our friends every once in a while; make dinner for the family; ask our neighbor how she is doing. Why? Because sometimes, relationships are built purely on those who show up and try to make it work. What we have may not be what we want, but it will never grow if we are never around to let it.

The same was true for my relationship with God. When I started showing up, even when I did not want to, I found myself growing closer to him. There was a bond being formed, a part of me that began to look forward to our time together. At times, I even began to feel God *calling* me to prayer. I will never forget one such occasion. For whatever reason, I decided to stay up late with some brothers and went to bed thinking that I might just sleep in the next day. What's just one day missed? I intentionally did not set my alarm because I knew that I would just be too tired. The next morning, I not only woke up without the alarm at the exact time I normally did for my private prayer, I found myself wide awake (a true miracle for anyone who has seen me in the morning!) God—I felt in that moment—was not going to accept any excuse I placed between us, and had taken it upon himself to remove every barrier in my way. God had prepared a path and was inviting me to walk it. What could I do but get out of bed and go pray?

A year after my initial personal encounter with Jesus, I found that my relationship with God was growing: Not only was I encountering God, I was beginning to see him as the strength and foundation of my life. What started from a sense of duty, the compulsion to fulfill an obligation, was now finding its purpose in a sense of fidelity, a desire to be faithful and true to the one I loved and needed.

And there it was. A shift in my prayer and relationship to God, simply as a result of showing up: I realized in a new and profound way that I *loved* God, without quotations this time, and that I *needed* God. I will never forget the words that a close friar friend and mentor told me prior to starting the year. He said, "The purpose of this year, beyond all else, is to realize that Jesus is the only one you will ever find in your life who will never let you down. The brothers will let you down. The Church will let you down. You, even, will let yourself down. But Jesus, Jesus will never *ever* let you down. Learn, with all your heart, to trust in him and him alone." Prior to the year starting, these words were just good advice. At the end of the year, they were beginning to become a reality. While I had a *long* way to go—excuse me—while *I still have* a long way to go in being faithful to God and in trusting in him above all us, the foundation had been laid. In times of trial, I knew of no other place I would go.

Which was good. Because once I found myself out of novitiate and back in the real world, working for the Church and trying to "save the world," the initial words of my formator became very true: The foundation that I had laid was about to determine the rest of my life as a friar. In times of trial, what was I going to have to rely on? As I recounted during my internship year at a parish, I found, somewhat to my surprise, that the grace of God was all I needed when life came crashing down.

A Thorn in My Side

Over the past three or four weeks, I've experienced a fair amount of disappointment. From the trivial (watching a favorite sports team's season go up in flames; giving up on a failed video project after many hours of work) to the substantial (realizing that major parts of my internship year plan are no longer possible; attending a heart-wrenching funeral), and everything in between (being yelled at by parishioners on separate occasions over the election; having plans to see close friends cancelled because of Hurricane Matthew; feeling a few close relationships slip away), it has been a difficult month at times. While there have been some tremendous moments as well, and overall, these moments of disappointment pale in comparison to the tragedies that many have to go through each day around the world, there is no denying that the lows for me lately have been lower than normal. Having been shaken out of the normal routine and forced to deal with unwanted situations instead, there is a strong sense of uneasiness in my life now as I walk on uneven ground.

And yet, in this same time, I have also experienced a sense of confidence and clarity that I haven't felt in a long time. When many things around me have wavered, my prayer life has flourished.

As my close friends and longtime followers know, I am someone with great ambition. I am wired in such a way that I am constantly looking to the future, setting goals, and finding ways to accomplish things that are important to me. As much as I know that the world is absolutely not a meritocracy, there is something deep inside me that believes that I can accomplish anything I want with enough effort, and that, because I'm a "good person" and work hard, my life will ultimately be filled with success and good things. In essence, I can control my fate if I work hard enough.

Ha!

When said like that, such a sentiment is obviously ridiculous. Of course I can't control my own fate. Of course I need God in my life because God is my all and the reason for everything good in my life. And yet, when things are going well, these things are easy to forget. My faith formation classes are successful because I'm a good teacher. *Duh!* My relationships are healthy and fruitful because I'm mature and self-giving. *Naturally!* Things in my life go as planned because I think ahead and work hard. *If only others were like me!* Even though there's not one of us who would say that God is not the most important part of our lives and the ultimate reason for our successes, when things are going well, it's very easy to see oneself as the impetus of one's success, and not turn to God with the same longing.

Not in times of trial. Not over the past three to four weeks for me. No, when standing on uneven ground, when the world has been shaken up and we find things well outside of the norm, the focus and intent of prayer changes dramatically. We begin to actually believe what we say, realizing that there is no one greater than our God, no good thing that doesn't come from Him, and truly nothing else that matters.

I think St. Paul captures this sentiment perfectly in his second letter to the Corinthians in describing his many trials:

"That I might not become too elated, a thorn in the flesh was given to me, an angel of Satan, to beat me, to keep me from being too elated. Three times I begged the Lord about this, that it might leave me, but he said to me, 'My grace is sufficient for you, for power is made perfect in weakness.' I will rather boast most gladly of my weaknesses, in order that the power of Christ may dwell with me. Therefore, I am content with weaknesses, insults, hardships, persecutions, and constraints, for the sake of Christ; for when I am weak, then I am strong." (2 Cor. 12:7-10)

The beauty of this passage is not that he prayed to God and God gave him what he needed, it's that he came to realize that faith in God is not dependent on one's current situation, good or bad. Sometimes God not answering his prayer to remove his suffering sounds harsh, but it was probably the best thing for him: Had God simply answered his prayer and took his suffering away, Paul might have continued to judge the sufficiency and meaningfulness of his life on the things around him. My life is good because things are going well. Instead, having to deal with weakness, he came to realize that his life is good because God has given him grace... because the power of Christ dwells in him. It is this, not the external blessings or hardships, that makes one's life meaningful. It is in giving up one's desire to be Lord, that futile attempt to control everything, that he came to realize who was really in control and had the strength he needed.

This has precisely been my experience of late. By no means has my life been worthy of its own *Lifetime Original Movie,* but there has no doubt been a little turbulence. My plans have not exactly panned out the way I had hoped and I have come to realize (once again) that I am not strong enough to make everything go well in life. And I'm extremely happy because of this. In having to face disappointment and accept that there are things outside of my control that I will just have to deal with, my dependence on God and commitment to this relationship has strengthened considerably. Taking these issues to God in prayer—the trivial, significant and everything in between—I have begun to care less about the issues themselves as a gauge for my life, and begun to gain much more satisfaction in the one who truly matters, our God. I know that I cannot control everything (or anything) in life, but I surely know that God's grace is enough. It is only with a thorn in one's side that we can truly know this.

In times of trial, all our theories and nice language are put to the test. While in novitiate it was great to say, "My God and my all, what more could I ever want in life?" There was no real desperation or need to test it. What about when God does not seem as close to me anymore, when my strength and protector seems distant and unreliable? In sports, when a team is doing well and being complimented for having such great chemistry with each other, the wise coach always says, "Yeah, but let's see how they do when they lose a couple of games." With stress, pressure, failure, and disappointment, our true selves come out, and we find out what truly matters. In trial, it is very easy to let our relationship slip, to let the worries of the world overwhelm us and take us from our source of strength. It can even become very easy to *blame* God—and understandably so—for not being the protector and guardian in which we have put all our trust. *Where were you, God, when things were going so poorly for me? Why didn't you stop it from happening?*

This was not the case for me. For whatever reason, I knew that God was closer than ever. In my time of trial, I did not run from God, I found greater refuge and strength in him than I ever did in times of prosperity. I *had* to pray, not because of compulsion or duty, but because it was the only source of strength that could actually get me through it. Jesus truly was the only one in my life that would never let me down, the only one who would always support me, and so I found refuge in him first and foremost.

With such a powerful statement of faith and clear benefits of prayer, it may be tempting to stop the story right there. It would be easy to see how some would say that this is the moment when prayer reaches its pinnacle. When we realize that we are weak and so begin to rely on God for everything we need, there is nothing greater; we have achieved a satisfying and fulfilling prayer life.

And in a way, yes. That is no small feat, by any stretch.

But I think it is only telling half of the story. As important as prayer is in our lives as a source of strength and purpose, prayer is much more than just a therapeutic process, and God is much more than our metaphysical teddy bear that gives us all that we need. When we enter into a meaningful relationship with the God of all that is good, we do not do so primarily to achieve *our* goals, we do so to achieve *God's*. True prayer, it would seem then, is not focused on convincing God to be more like us, but *in making us more like God*. Prayer, in its fullness, does give us strength and purpose for our journey, but it also challenges us to conversion and reroutes the very journey we think we are on. As I recounted after my hermitage retreat during postulancy, wanting to be closer to God often means identifying and removing the barriers we knowingly or unknowingly place between us.

This Moment is Sufficient

Do you have any idea how quiet, quiet can be when there's nothing to do but sit and listen? Better yet, do you have any idea how much there is to hear/feel/understand/know when you're still enough to let it happen? It's dangerous, I tell you!

In the stillness of the moment, I was reminded of two people that I had neither spoken to nor thought about in years. What makes these individuals special is that they hurt me in a profound way a long time ago, and I have bottled my resentment towards them ever since, never seeking to let go or to seek reconciliation. Only when my heart was still enough to hear God did I realize that my subconscious bitterness toward both of them had been stinting my relationship with God, and that it was time for me to "unclench my fist" so to speak. Was it possible for me to love God while hating my brother? I asked myself. Providentially, the Gospel at Mass that afternoon was The Parable of the Unforgiving Servant (Matthew 18:21-35), a Gospel that gave me a pretty good answer. Without the openness to be still, I would have never heard it in the way I needed to hear it.

Which brings me to the culminating point of this post: This moment is sufficient. Unlike in our Western, capitalistic society in which we've been trained to want more and to work to achieve more in the future, God offers everything that we could ever possibly want in each present moment: Himself. As C.S. Lewis correctly points out in *The Screwtape Letters,* "The present is the point at which time touches eternity" (#15). To be more concerned with future possibilities than with present realities is to implicitly accept a false existence, a construct of our own imaginations that bears only a semblance of truth, over the concrete Truth presented to us by God in this moment alone. While we should always remain hopeful for the future, and plan for it in the sense that we will be open to the new possibilities that God may provide, to allow either of these to distract us from the fullness of God's presence in our lives in this very moment is utterly useless. When I was still enough to listen, I realized that there's nothing I need to be left wanting for. In this moment, I can know God.

This time, when I was silent enough in prayer to listen, still enough to allow God to be present to me and me to God, I found myself uncovering answers to questions I did not know I even had. There, working under the surface of who I had projected myself to be were a lot of feelings and thoughts I was unaware of. Resentment. Pain. Anger. Regret. Something inside of me was pulling me away from what I should have wanted—forgiveness, humility, and reconciliation—and toward what I did not want: revenge and personal justice. When I stopped looking outward and began to take a look inside, God helped me to see that the path my heart was on was not the path of the Gospel; what I desired was not what God desired. When I entered into the moment and gave up everything but a desire to be with God, I understood that I needed to change.

If you ask me, therein lies the true grace of prayer.

As much as prayer can be empowering and offer the strength to continue on in life, an opportunity for us to voice our needs and afflictions to God, it can often go awry if that is all it is. For many in the modern world, religion and a belief in God are simply projections of ourselves, the fulfillment of our every desire. Rather than God creating humanity in his image, critics of religion say that we, the believers, have actually created God in our image. And who can disagree with them if our prayer is nothing more than a self-affirmation of what we want to hear, a source of strength that emboldens us to do only what we want to do? Sadly, those critics of religion and faith have a point in these situations: When our "God" gives us the strength to hate, divide, conquer, dehumanize, exclude, and cause pain, to carry out selfish desires that benefit us rather than building up the kingdom of God with inclusivity, love, and reconciliation, *we are not praying to the living and true God of Christianity.* Something is tragically missing.

In its fullness, prayer is an encounter with God that *transforms* the way we see and interact with the world. As so many saints and theologians have suggested, it is like a bright light that reveals what we otherwise do not see: When we wear glasses or look through a window away from the light, we can believe that the glass is perfectly clean. But turn our perspective and hold it up to the light, all of a sudden we are able to see smudges, scratches, and cracks that have been there all along but completely hidden to our normal consciousness. *That* is the effect that an encounter with God can have on our lives. When we stop for a moment the desire to convince God to give us what we want and simply encounter God in Godself—to aim our full attention at the light itself rather than using it to see what we want—our focus becomes clear. All of a sudden, we see ourselves and the world the way God does… and for the first time know that things are not the way that the should be. Something needs to change.

Often, that something is us.

This insight was never clearer to me than in 2015 after yet another mass shooting in the United States that claimed many lives. As is often the case, politicians and celebrities shared their condolences and prayers publicly. And it angered me. More than any time before, it became clear to me that *true* prayer, prayer as I had experienced it on my retreat and that forced me to change parts of my life, was not at work. True prayer, as I wrote in this post, called us to more.

Prayers Are Not Enough

In the wake of the 355th mass shooting—of this year—many politicians sent out condolences in the form of prayers to the people of San Bernadino, CA. Things like, "Our thoughts and prayers go out to the victims of this tragedy," and "Praying for peace and safety for our first responders today," were in high number. And there's nothing wrong with either of these statements: My thoughts and prayers were also focused on those affected by the tragedy, and I too was concerned for the first responders who were putting themselves in danger. These are great sentiments for sure.

And yet, prayers like these have caused quite the outrage in recent months. After the mass shooting at Umpqua Community College on October 1 of this year (at that point, we had only had 294 mass shootings in 274 days), President Obama emphatically remarked, "Our thoughts and prayers are not enough. It's not enough. It does not capture the heartache and grief we should feel, and it does nothing to prevent this carnage being repeated somewhere else in America." Today, the New York *Daily News* responded in a similar way with the headline, "God Isn't Fixing This," calling a number of politicians "cowards" for their "meaningless platitudes." In both cases, as with the many people who have suffered at the hands of gun violence, there seems to be a growing dissatisfaction with the prayer. We cannot depend on God to fix all of our problems, many say. We need to do something ourselves.

What do we as Christians make of this?

In each of these cases—the politicians who tweeted their condolences, President Obama calling for more than prayer, and the NY *Daily News* calling for anything but prayer—"prayer" is understood in a rather narrow, private, and disconnected sense. When we pray, it seems to all of them, we present desires or wishes to something or someone outside of ourselves in hopes that they will be granted. In this sense, prayer is a way of expressing what it is most important to an individual, and for those who "believe in the power of prayer," it offers a sense of comfort that everything will ultimately be all right; God listens to and answers our prayers, we say and believe, so this many people praying must work out in the long run, right?

But I'm not convinced that this is the definition of prayer that we want to rest on. While, yes, intercessory prayer is definitely a component of a full prayer life, by itself, understood as it has been presented, it is a tragically incomplete experience.

Think of it this way. If God is eternal, perfect, and unchanging, how is it that we can change God's mind about something so as to cause God to intervene? (We can't!) There is no possible desire or request that we could ever express that God doesn't already know, hasn't been thinking about for all eternity, and is currently intervening to the extent God sees fit (how and why God intervenes is a topic for another post...) We may ask for something, but God already knows what's best for us and will give us all that we need when we need it. In other words, our prayers do not change God's mind or control God's actions.

For some, it may sound like I'm saying that we should abandon all intercessory prayer. "If God doesn't change, why even ask for help? God's going to do what God's going to do with or without my prayer." In a way, yes, this is true: God cannot be "moved" by anything outside of Godself. But that doesn't mean I'm saying we shouldn't seek God's intercession... it means that we should understand prayer in a deeper way. Instead of thinking about prayer as a way for us to change God, why not see it as a opportunity for God to change us?

You see, prayer is more than a one-way communication of "pleases" and "thank-yous" in which we speak and God chooses to answer or not; it is a multi-directional, active experience of God in which we not only communicate our desires or emotions to God, God communicates with us in such a way to transform, convert, and inspire the very desires and emotions we share. Prayer is not a time in which God listens patiently and conforms to our desires (ha!), it is the time when we open ourselves up enough to listen patiently to God and conform ourselves to God's desires. In other words, prayer is an experience that makes us more like God, not God more like us.

If this is our understanding of prayer—getting back to politicians dealing with our tragic situation of repeated gun violence— true prayer is not an expression of our sentiments or a way to express our condolences, it is an act that gives us the clarity and motivation to act more like God in the world. True prayer is transformative. It does not end when we say "Amen" and go about the rest of our day. That's when the prayer truly begins.

And so, while I find the president's speech lacking in nuance and the news article misunderstanding the role that prayer can play, their frustrations are rightly directed: "Prayer" that does not result in a new way of thinking or acting, that does not seek to reconcile the situation or prevent new tragedies from occurring, is far from the experience that it can and should be. Prayers by politicians that are accompanied by inaction, or worse, action that deliberately works against the prevention of more tragedies, are not enough.

Of all the homilies I have ever heard, I will never forget the one preached on the feast of the Ascension during my first year with the friars. Evoking memories of being a child, the priest recalled how he loved to sit in the back seat while his parents drove. There he would sit, in complete comfort and without any responsibility, knowing that his parents would care for him. This reminded him of life in the Church growing up, a time when lay people were called on to do nothing more than "pray, pay, and obey," to comfortably sit in the back seat without meaningful responsibility knowing that the priests and bishops would care for the Church. And so it was in the life of the disciples when Jesus walked the earth: With Jesus leading the way, they could rest in comfort without any real responsibility because they knew that Jesus would take care of the mission.

But then something changed.

One day, he grew up and had to take care of himself. One day, the Church at the Second Vatican Council restored the primacy of baptism in Christian life and called for the full participation of all the faithful in the life of the Church. One day, Jesus returned to the Father and gave his disciples his Holy Spirit, entrusting them with the power and authority to lead the mission. No longer in the back seat, no longer incapable of doing something for themselves, they all faced the uncomfortable reality that *they* were responsible now. No one was going to *do it for them.* Emboldened by the Spirit dwelling in them, they came to understand that they had the power to carry out the will of God on earth, to be co-creators with Christ in building up the kingdom. How could they sit in the back any longer? How can we?

When I think back to why I was so angry with the politicians and celebrities "praying" for the victims but unwilling to change anything about our society to prevent tragedies from happening in the future, it is this homily that comes to mind. Prayer is not some casual encounter with an external and unknowable genie in which we make our needs known and then go about living our normal lives, comfortable and without responsibility. No! Prayer is an intimate and life-changing relationship, one in which we find that the living and true God, the creator and reconciler of all that exists, is closer to us than we are to ourselves, already dwelling within us and forming all that we think and do in the world. Because of this, we find within us all the capability and responsibility to build the kingdom of God in our midst, that the answer to our prayers is not to be found in some far off heaven or carried out in some extraordinary miracle: The miracle is in us. *We are God's hands and feet. We are God's mouth and ears.* To request something from this God and remain unchanged by it is a contradiction within our very selves! True prayer—that is, encounters with the God dwelling deep within us—naturally and necessarily leads us to become the very thing we desire, *changing the world* as we know it.

And with that, we find ourselves back where we started. Prior to joining the friars six years ago, all I could see was the outward effects of their inner lives. I saw men who had made it their life's goal to stand up for justice, to remember the forgotten, to reconcile the estranged, and to heal the broken. I saw men who were changing the world. What they did, I wanted to do, and I did not want to wait to get started. As far as I was concerned, I was ready.

But of course, I was not ready. Beneath the outward enthusiasm and work ethic that these men showed, at the root of their joy and perseverance in a difficult life, was something that I could not see and had yet to understand: They were not guided by good intentions and their work was not built on their own strength, but rather on a strong foundation of prayer with God. It was God, who in the silence of their lives, had called them to do what they may not have originally wanted to do; had challenged them to go where they would not have chosen to go on their own; had inspired them with enthusiasm and strength to believe that they could actually make a difference; and had comforted them in failure when their efforts did not immediately bring about the kingdom of heaven before their eyes. While I was inspired by their lives and work and felt that I could immediately imitate what they did—and maybe for a short time I could have—I did not yet possess what made their lives possible: the intimate relationship with God only found in silence.

To spend so much time doing essentially *nothing*, consistently disconnecting from the world and all its needs to sit silently, without any objective, any response, any effect, or any way of evaluating progress is absolutely ludicrous when there is so much we could be doing to *change the world*. The me of six years ago could not understand this and the me of today is far from mastering it. And yet, now that I have entered the silence and heard what I did not think was there, now that I have felt the living God within me and begun a relationship of love and respect, I know that nothing in this world would be possible without it. Despite all we do as friars in our external lives, I have come to embrace the fact that we are, at our very core and above all else, men of prayer.

. . . . . .

chapter **three**

_____

A Life to Share

A seminary professor of mine used to say that no matter who
you are or where you are from, becoming an adult requires
that we answer two simple, yet fundamental questions of life:
Does my life have meaning? and _Who is going to love me?_
As much as beauty, wealth, status, and personal achievement
serve as markers to the world of a happy and successful life,
they remain but symptoms and effects of our much deeper
desires and can never fully satisfy us in themselves. At our
core, all we truly want is to know that our life matters and
that someone loves us.

In a sense, we know as Christians that the answer to both of
these questions resides in one place: a relationship with God.
Nowhere else will we find greater meaning. In no one else will
we find greater love. When we rest in God and keep him as
our central focus, the most important questions of our very
existence can be confidently answered and we can live without
worry.

In another sense, however, we know as Christians that we
are not simply spiritual beings who live in eternity without any
needs: In our earthly lives we are embodied spirits living in a
physical, temporal world. While we may not spiritually need

anything more than God in our lives and may even be content saying that God is all we need to answer the first question, when it comes to knowing who will love us, physically we are social, corporeal beings that need to be in relationship with one another. Even the most powerful and life-giving experience with God cannot replace our human desire to love and be loved by others. In fact, I would go as far as to say that such a relationship with God is not even possible unless we know what it means to love and be loved by others. How can we speak of a relationship with God and use words like *love*, *trust, compassion*, and *sacrifice* if these words do not first find meaning in our human experience? Our entire experience of God, says St. John, is rooted in the way we treat each other: "No one has ever seen God. Yet, *if we love one another*, God remains in us, and his love is brought to perfection in us" (1 John 4:12; emphasis mine). As much as we know in our heart that God loves us and as much consolation that might bring at times, we also know that we could never experience the fullness of that love in complete solitude. We need to be in relationship with others.

And so, *who is going to love me?*

For the vast majority of people, the answer to this question is an exclusive, romantic partner with whom we can make a family and grow old. A soul mate, as it were. While the love we receive from our parents and those who raise us is irreplaceable, and the love we find in our closest friends can last a lifetime, there is no matching the intensity of a soul mate. In this one person is our best friend, our companion on the journey, strength in difficult times, delight in joyful times, and of course, our romantic partner. For many, there is nothing greater to be sought in all of life and no one greater to be loved by. A soul mate completes us.

Now, ignoring for the purpose of my story any question about whether such a person exists, whether it is healthy to concentrate all of one's interpersonal needs on a single person, or if such romantic expectations may actually diminish a full experience of love by replacing God with another person... I can say for sure that the desire to find one's soul mate is really important to most, and *really* a deterrent for a life that requires celibate chastity! When we are brought up thinking that the source of our intimacy is found in a single other person, that the happiest moment of our life is in marrying that person, and that—based on the advertising of every product in civilization—sex is the greatest thing ever discovered and should be sought as frequently as possible, there is not going to be a long line to sign up for religious life or the priesthood. I cannot say that I have any hard data to support it, but in my experience—both in discernment and in speaking with young men and women over the past decade—celibacy is the number one deterrent to a vocation.

But notice how I said "celibacy" (remaining unmarried) and not "chastity" (living out one's sexuality in an appropriate way). As much as the desire for sex is a powerful force in deterring young men and women to take up this way of life, I do not honestly think that it is the fundamental obstacle. As I wrote during my first year with the friars, I found in my own discernment and in talking to others that, while the prospect of not having sex was a bit unfortunate, the fear of being lonely was overwhelming. If so much of life is about answering the question *who is going to love me*, then how do I answer that question without a soul mate?

A Life to Share

Celibacy can be a bit of a deal-breaker. Ask any young Catholic man or woman, active in their faith, why they are not considering some form of consecrated life, and I can almost guarantee that celibacy is one of the reasons. "I really want to get married," you might hear. From my own experience, this was the largest hurdle to jump.

But despite what many may think, including even those going through the discernment process, I don't believe that the problem is abstinence from sex (at least not entirely). Believe it or not, there are still many young people in this world who have not discarded chastity for the loose sexuality embraced by popular culture. (It's not what you hear on TV or see in the movies, but it's still out there, trust me!) And yet, of those who have held onto or readopted this unpopular virtue, there is an even smaller minority of people wishing to do so in the form of consecrated life. Why is this?

The reason has everything to do with intimacy, or rather, the perceived lack of intimacy in religious life. When I look back to the time when I used "I really wanted to get married" as an excuse, I believe what I was saying was, "I really want someone to share my life with." For much of my life, I saw marriage as the only way to do this. When I looked at the priests and religious I knew (which was only a few), all I saw were people growing in age, living alone, and frankly, looking either miserable or lonely. From this narrow experience I concluded that it must take the type of holy person that is willing to sacrifice any chance of intimacy for the sake of a worthwhile ministry, and I knew I was not that holy person.

The first step in my transformative move toward religious life was a painful, yet inevitable one: I matured. As I grew older and developed emotionally, I began to form relationships that were much more meaningful than being "just friends" while being wholly different from my romantic partners. I had begun to realize that intimacy was much more than just romance. For an adult, this is painstakingly obvious. But for me, the realization that I could be fulfilled and sustained emotionally, spiritually, intellectually, and even physically (in a different way of course) from something other than an exclusive, romantic relationship, meant that I didn't need to get married to have all of my needs met. It was not until this realization did the prospect of entering religious life even deserve my attention.

At some point, however, it did, and I was forced on an excruciating journey of heart and soul that tore me into pieces for many months. Can I do that sort of work? What about my girlfriend? Do I want children? Which community? Have I lived enough to know? Little by little I grew more comfortable with the idea, developed a fondness for St. Francis, and came to accept almost every aspect of Franciscan life. I could do that.

There remained one final question: Were these specific guys, the members of the Franciscan Friars of the Holy Name Province, guys that I wanted to share my life with? It's one thing to understand and to like the idea of fraternity in the way St. Francis instituted it, but another thing entirely to live it with actual people. I was convinced that religious life could fulfill me in the way I sought. But would it?

The long and short of it is a resounding yes. As I've come to know many of the men in this province over the past five years, I have felt a distinct growth in many of them from mere acquaintances, to familiar friends, to something potentially much more. While I'm growing to understand each member as a brother owed my unconditional love and respect, I have nonetheless grown close to a few in a very spectacular way. I find myself catching glimpses of an intimacy with my brothers that is to come, fulfilling and sustaining me for whatever lies in the road ahead.

It may be true that I will never be fulfilled in such a physical way that a wife could provide: I am never going to have sex. Frankly, I'll survive without it. But when I begin to look at celibacy through the lens I've described above, the abstinence from sex no longer appears to me as a restriction to be followed or a sacrifice to be endured; rather, it is the freedom, and the call to love more broadly than would ever be possible while vowed to just one person. I know that I feel called to this life, and that it is a life to share.

When so much of our societal framework is connected with romantic love and sex, it can be difficult for outsiders to understand why anyone would join this life. On the one hand, there are those for whom the whole thing makes absolutely no sense, and they are dissatisfied with the practice of celibacy in principle. On more than a few occasions, both in discernment and even as a friar, people have looked at me completely puzzled and asked, "But don't you want to get married? Have kids?" The thought of giving such things up, no matter the reason, seems ludicrous and unconscionable. Clearly, something must be wrong with me. There are also those on the other side of the spectrum, those who look upon us with tremendous admiration and say things like, "What an amazing sacrifice you've made!" Knowing, of course, the great need in the Church and amazed at what we do, they want to applaud us for all that we have given up to do it. Unfortunately, even though this may seem positive at first, they are just as misled as the former group. You see, at the heart of both examples is a belief that we have chosen a life without love to do what we are doing. Believing that we continue to hold to the values of the world, that is, that finding a soul mate is the greatest form of love and should be desired above all else, our life is either "amazing" or makes no sense because we have chosen to deny ourselves—that is, to give up what we really wanted—to serve the Lord.

While this may be the case for others, and there was certainly a generation of priests and religious that understood their vows as nothing more than the hoops one needed to jump through to do the work of God, *this is not true for me in the slightest.* I say, even if there was no longer a law requiring celibacy for priests, even if I could live as a married, ordained man in the Catholic Church, I would remain a vowed Franciscan brother who lives a chaste, celibate life. Seriously. The reason for this—and what is truly at the heart of this whole chapter—is that I have chosen this life not to *escape* love or *despite* my desire to be married, but because I have found the most profound way to live for nothing *but* love. I have chosen to live a chaste, celibate life in fraternity because it answers one of the most important questions of being an adult. *Who is going to love me?* God and my brothers. For me, this life offers more than any single soul mate could.

I remember back in my discernment I was particularly worried about what my life would be like in old age in a community such as this, without a soul mate or children by my side. Would I one day feel lonely? Would my life still have meaning? I sat down for breakfast one morning during a stay with some of the friars and one of the older brothers started to the others, "Did I ever tell you the story about…" Before he could finish, the rest of the table, in unison, groaned back, "Yes... we have heard *all* of your stories." Giving him a hard time in jest, of course, they all laughed, but the brother was completely undeterred. "Well, fine, you ingrates. *He* [me] hasn't heard this one so I'm going to tell it anyway." There, at more than eighty years old, was a man surrounded by brothers who loved him, joked with him, and continued to challenge him, a group of men with whom he could laugh, find comfort in distress, and share his life. This brother was not lonely in the slightest.

And neither am I.

All around me are men who share my ideals for life, who want to make the world a better place, and who want God to be at the center of it all. Nowhere else in my life have I laughed with such freedom and abandon than with the brothers around the dinner table; nowhere else have I had such engaging and stimulating conversations about faith and our world than with the brothers late at night; nowhere else in the world have I felt the comfort and support to be vulnerable about who I am and what I need than with the brothers in private conversations. In this fraternity, the brotherhood of prayer and service to the world, are hundreds (thousands, worldwide) of men who will love me—and allow me to love them—in good times and in bad, in sickness and in health, 'til death do us part, to be intimate partners throughout our lives. Truly, in the brothers, I find my solid floor, the foundation that holds me up and never lets me fall too low.

If only the story ended here...

It can be tempting to stop here on the surface, to remain where it is easy and comforting, where fraternity is nothing more than the group of people that supports me. But we cannot stop here. To end on such a simple and unchallenged note, to imply that what makes fraternal life meaningful is that we all like and support each other, is not only grossly misleading, it leaves out the most meaningful part of living together: giving up part of ourselves to build something greater. A big part of fraternal life—as I shared while on summer assignment in 2015—is coming to terms with the fact that even though we could do everything exactly the way we wanted on our own, struggling to work together is often more rewarding.

You Can Be as Poor as You Want

I have mentioned a number of times that Franciscan poverty, freeing oneself of material possessions in order to identify with the poor Jesus, was a major attraction to me in my discernment; receiving a minor in Poverty Studies and completing an internship at a soup kitchen even before seriously considering the friars should tell a bit about me. I have also mentioned that defining Franciscan poverty has been an eight-hundred-year battle among Franciscans; what and how much one should be able to own has been fought over and divided the charism more than a few times.

In response to this (and the problems particular to our province of men in the twenty-first century), a number of our friars have taken the opinion that a friar "can be as poor as he wants in this province." What they mean by this is that one's personal decisions for a simpler lifestyle are one's own free choice. No one is forcing us to spend any of our stipend, maintain excessive wardrobes, or consume any more food or drink than we want. Even if others define poverty in an altogether different way and live much more comfortably than one would choose, their decisions, these friars would say, do not affect their ability to live their own brand of poverty: You can be as poor as you want.

Over the past four years I've thought about and struggled to live out this opinion. There is great truth in it: Why blame others or "the culture of the friars" for not living poorly enough when I take everything that's given to me without question? I have been forced (in a very good way) to think about what I've been given by the friars and decide if that's even too much. At times, it has meant giving back part of my stipend, abstaining from food or drink, and refusing gifts. And that helps. But I find that this is only part of the answer. When we choose to live together, whether that be in a Franciscan context, a family, or simply in a larger society, we are never free to do anything and everything we want.

It's tough to be that poor in America. Having just spent ten days in one of the poorest countries in the Western Hemisphere, I have now seen real poverty (as compared to the "poverty" we Franciscans live.) I saw houses the size of the bedroom I'm in right now with dirt floors and little-to-no sanitation, teenagers that walk two hours each way to get an education, children that had to drop out of school to help support their families, and meals in which a tortilla is the main (or only) item on the menu. Compared to even the poorest in the United States, the average person in Nicaragua has very little.

And yet, there is a great appeal to the simplicity of lifestyle we saw. Sure, they had much less, but their world was not tied to material possessions in the way that ours is. Most of them had very little, but many of them had a sufficient amount, and were happy. It's no wonder that so many people go on trips like these and have a great desire to change their lives when they come home. Looking at the excesses all around them in the US, people like me, feel very uncomfortable with all the things they now see as luxuries.

But good luck getting rid of them. What I mean by this is not a cynical take on one's ability to let go, but rather a realization that much of what we have is built into our social structure. Are we really going to renounce clean drinking water to be in solidarity with our poor brothers and sisters in Nicaragua? Are we really going to throw our toilet paper in the trashcan rather than flushing it to go through some of the hardships they do? Are we really going to turn off our air conditioners and lobby that every other home and business we visit do the same so we can experience the relentless heat we knew there? I don't think so. They're kind of ridiculous questions, really. But that's the point. So many of our luxuries are built into our societal structure and are outside of our control. Short of doing these radically ridiculous things, we are not free to live as poorly as we want.

Living together means shared decisions. Bringing this question back to where it started— the Franciscan friary—we can see a similar dynamic. One's personal decisions can affect the situation, to an extent, but are not the only factor in the situation. What if others in the house don't agree with one's conception of poverty? What if everyone in the house has a different conception? I may think it inappropriate to ever eat filet mignon as a friar (hypothetical), while others might think it's appropriate sometimes, and even more think that it's appropriate often. Does the house eat filet mignon? My personal desires only go so far in community because, believe it or not, there are other personal desires than mine. I would obviously be free to abstain from eating the steak as it is outside of my conception of poverty and no one can force me to eat it. True. I could go make a PB and J sandwich and be completely happy. But look what I have done: I have decided that my personal desire is great enough that I'm willing to remove myself from the group to do my own thing. I have chosen that it is better to be "right" than to be "together."

And maybe, at times, that's what we have to do. Everyone can't be happy all the time, and I don't mind abstaining for someone else's happiness. For one meal, that's no big deal. But what if it's every meal? What if it's every friar outing? What if it's the general life of the friary? I can abstain from eating certain meals, but I cannot abstain from living in a certain house or using certain furniture. Just as in the situation with Nicaragua, there is a clear sense of culture in each friary that cannot be discounted. It is something outside any one person's control and has a great effect on his ability to act how he wants.

So, can you be as poor as you want as a friar? No, not at all. And I struggle with that. But it's a struggle I want to have because I am not called to be a king. I am not called to be right all of the time and to get my way. I am called as a Franciscan to a humble life in community in which I have to learn to accept my brothers' desires as legitimate, to grow outside of myself, and to live with the poverty that I am not in control. Sometimes, as difficult as it may sound, I have to compromise on my own ideals for the sake of community. Does this mean that I'm a fraud, that I'm weak and a hypocrite because I don't stand up for what I believe? No. It means that, while I will challenge my brothers to a simpler lifestyle when I can, I realized very early in my Franciscan life that we are called to be together, not necessarily always "right." A big part of being Franciscan is realizing that community life is never going to be exactly how we envision it, but that it is better to be challenged by our brothers than to easily have everything we want on our own. In this way, I know that on my own I could live more materially poor and in better keeping with my own sense of simple living, but it is only in community that I can experience the poverty of not being in control and having to work with others

that are different from you. In this sense—and maybe only in this
sense—you can can be as poor as you want.

There is a classic story that I love to tell about a man who
died and ended up in the the most idyllic world imaginable.
All around were people like him and who liked him, and he
never once had a fight with anyone; if there was a disagreement, the others always took his side. Each day he was free
to indulge in anything he wanted without any consequences
or ill effects; he played poker and always won, he drank his
favorite whiskey and never got drunk, and at the end of the
night, always managed to get the girl. Never once did anyone
go against him, never once was anything out of place.

At some point, the man began to grow tired of such constant
gratification. Surrounded only by those who supported him
no matter what he did, successful no matter how hard he tried
to fail, and completely unchallenged against his own selfish
desires, the excitement of everything he used to love faded.
He went to the angel and requested a transfer: "This heaven
of yours is quite nice, but it is a little boring. I think I might
try hell for a little while. Maybe there I will be able to feel
something again."

The angel replied, "Oh, I am terribly sorry, sir. This *is* hell."

When I lived in the world, I was the king of my own life.
I chose when I would eat, when I would sleep, with whom
I would associate, how I would spend my money, and what
activities I would do. While obviously never the complete
and only determiner of my circumstances, I essentially had
the freedom to do as I pleased. If I did not like someone, I
could exclude them from my life. If something was painful or

uncomfortable, I could just avoid it. In other words, my life was largely determined by what I did or did not want, and I sought an idyllic world just like the man in the story.

I was the king, and I liked that—for a while.

But I am not called to be a king. As a Christian, a pilgrim in this world, my goal is not to rule here on earth, it is to point to the heavenly kingdom we await. In that kingdom, we are not kings but servants. We do not decide what we will do, when we will do it, or most importantly, *with whom we will associate*; we live in communion with all as fellow elect, doing what needs to be done for the common good. There with us will not be only those who are like us or who did the same things we did on earth, but men and women from every culture, time, and social setting, with every interest, personality, and terrible idiosyncrasy. Dare I say, there with us will be some who lived far more saintly lives than we did and others who committed every sort of sin imaginable.

And at that point, none of it will matter.

Community life tries to mirror that kingdom, offering an example to a world full of kings of what our heavenly home will look like. While there will always be those in community like us and who like us, so much of our time is spent learning to love those who are different from us and dealing with those we cannot stand. We come from different families and different cultures, for different reasons, with different conceptions of what this life should be. How we define poverty is just the tip of the iceberg. What about prayer life? Ministry? Expectations of fraternal time? I do not think it is offensive or crass to say that we have in our brotherhood hundreds of men who, had they met in their previous lives, would never have associated with one another. Outside of religious life, they would probably want nothing to do with one another (and for some, maybe even *within* this life as well!) Not only is it an unfair expectation that a diverse group of men will become best friends, it is unfair to expect that there will not be major conflicts. Some guys, as hard as it is to believe given the commonality of life, simply do not get along.

And yet, *they try to make it work.*

This next post, written after a particularly difficult fraternal year, captures the great anguish—yet great fruit—that community life can bring when living with difficult people. On more than a few occasions throughout the year, I found myself frustrated, disappointed, and questioning my vocation, wondering how I could ever survive a life with the men around me. I began wishing that my fraternity was different, that the men I did not like would just leave and I could form a community only with those who were like me. Despite my best intentions, I had become the king once again, judging and dividing to build a kingdom pleasing to me. Then one day I realized something amazing: The kingdom that I sought was not *beyond* the mess of the fraternity, it was actually right there in the middle of it.

This Is Not What I Signed Up For!

There came a moment during this past year when the luster of novitiate began to fade, and community life became more of a burden than a joy. I'm not sure exactly what it was, but I looked around at the inane and constantly occurring conflicts in the friary, the unbearable idiosyncrasies of some of the strangest people you will ever meet, and the dysfunction of leadership that still struggles to understand and live the charism of our founder after eight hundred years of fighting, and just screamed, "This is not what I signed up for!" I signed up to be a part of a group of men that live, work, and pray together to bring about the kingdom of God; a group of men that identifies with and works for the poor and marginalized of society; a group of men that recognizes the wonder of creation, the power of the incarnation, and the joy of experiencing it all. *That's* what I signed up for.

That same week, I found a letter written by Fr. Jose Carballo, OFM, the former minister general of the Order of Friars Minor and the current secretary for the *Congregation for Institutes of Consecrated Life and Societies of Apostolic Life,* to the Poor Clares on their eight hundredth year anniversary. Fr. Carballo writes:

> If there is anything that destroys our fraternities it is the pretension of being above others, becoming judges of our brothers and sisters. This is due to our projecting onto them our dreams, and we demand of God and others that they fulfill them. Loving our dream of fraternity more than real fraternity, we turn into destroyers of fraternity. We begin to be accusers of our brothers, and then we accuse God, and finally we become desperate accusers of ourselves. We must remember that there will never exist the ideal fraternity that can accept our dreams of pretentious pride, and that the fraternity is built on the basis of pardon and reconciliation, since it has so much to do with our own limitations and those of others.

Obviously I knew that there would always be conflicts when it came to differing levels of cleanliness and work distribution, but when I searched further, I found that many of the things that frustrated me the most were not other people; they were the result of things that I brought to community life. Of the most notable was that I brought with me unfair expectations of others, exactly as Br. Carballo writes. Both consciously and subconsciously, I had determined how they should act, what they should believe in, what they should and shouldn't need. Because I was unable to be flexible with my expectations, they quickly turned into judgments, which turned into condemnations, eventually ending in resentment, something that did not leave me open to new experiences of love.

It was then that I found a book by Jean Vanier that described every feeling, thought, doubt, hope, and situation that I had experienced so far in novitiate. Entitled *Community and Growth: Our Pilgrimage Together,* Vanier offers insights and wisdom from his many years of founding communities that are both practical and spiritual. Here's how he opens the book:

> Community is a terrible place. [Good start, right?] It is the place where our limitations and our egoism are revealed to us. When we begin to live full-time with others, we discover our poverty and our weaknesses, our inability to get on with people, our mental and emotional blocks, our affective and sexual disturbances, our seemingly insatiable desires, our frustrations and jealousies, our hatred and our wish to destroy. While we were alone, we could believe we loved everyone. Now that we are with others, we realize how incapable we are of loving, how much we deny life to others. And if we become incapable of loving, what is left? There is nothing but blackness, despair and anguish. Love seems an illusion. We seem to be condemned to solitude and death.

> So community brings a painful revelation of our limitations, weaknesses and darkness; the unexpected discovery of the monsters within us is hard to accept. The immediate reaction is to try to destroy the monsters or to hide them away again,

pretending they don't exist, or to flee from community life and relationship with others, or to find that the monsters are theirs, not ours. But if we accept that monsters are there, we can let them out and learn to tame them. This is growth towards liberation.

These two texts were tremendously helpful in my formation this year, and I strongly recommend them to anyone entering community life. For me, they made me realize that what I was getting out of community life was in fact exactly what I signed up for. I signed up to be a penitent with men who recognize their limitations and sinfulness; men who bring with them brokenness and imperfection; men who realize that love is messy; men who know that it's worth getting on each others' nerves and letting each other down every once in a while if it means going through life together. I did not sign up to be in a group of perfect men without any need for God, nor did I sign up to be in a group of men exactly like me! Sure, there is a burden to community life some days, but in the end, even those burdens can be entirely grace-filled if you let them. Community life can definitely be a struggle, but I wouldn't have it any other way.

In times of frustration and disappointment, it can definitely be tempting to wish we were the king, that we were in the idyllic world where all the difficult people were banned, everyone did as we wanted, and everything went as we thought they should. If only we could pick the weeds ourselves, we think, prune away what is ugly and bothersome and leave only the good wheat in a perfectly manicured field, *then* things would be as they should be. Clearly, it is everyone else who has the problem, and once we get rid of them and make people more like us we can go about our business of focusing on what really matters: serving the people of God.

If only Jesus had not told us the opposite. If only it were *other people* with the problems.

In my friar life thus far, I have lived with more than a few brothers who seemed at first to share not a single thing in common with me, who lived by different values, worked for a different mission, and had presumably been sent by God for the sole purpose of annoying me. Oh, how I wish I could have shown them the door! And in my previous life, I could have. But not here. Here in this life, I am forced to engage the ones who are difficult for me, compelled to learn more about them and invite the into my life. Against every natural impulse I have, I am required to be nice to them and try to build something when nothing seems possible. I am required to let the weeds grow alongside the wheat and develop.

That is the way of the kingdom of God, and so that is the way of our fraternities.

And do you know what? Sometimes, relationships *do* actually form. Slowly, and not without difficulty, I have learned over the past six years how to love and respect some of the brothers who were most challenging to me at first. Sometimes, I have come to realize that it was *me* with the problem that needed fixing, that it was *me* who was causing so much frustration in another's life and *they* were the ones having patience! Time and time again I am utterly amazed by the transformation that can happen in communities and individuals—in myself—when we engage each other and work to move beyond our differences. Nowhere else is such an experience possible. Nowhere else in the world are people who cannot stand one another thrown together for life, told to make it work, *and do.*

For me, this is why I always tell people that the struggles of community life are more important and fulfilling than the joys. While support and encouragement are definitely benefits of being in community and the image of a solid floor is nice, I think that there is a more important image of fraternal life: a ceiling. When the brothers are around, we are not free to be king. Hanging over our heads to prevent us from getting too high is the constant reminder that we are not in charge. In our struggles with one another we are forced to recognize that other people and opinions around us—with all the baggage they bring—are just as important as *me* and *my* opinions and all the baggage *I* bring. Whereas when we were on our own we might have been tempted to get on our high horse and look down on others, with the ceiling over our heads, with the fraternity around us calling us out and keeping us in line, we will always be reminded of our place: We are humble friars that sit on the floor.

Sure, we could surround ourselves with only those that like us and who are like us and things would no doubt be easier. But which kingdom would we be pointing to if we did that? Only in the struggles—in the way that we treat one another and learn to overcome our differences—do we get a taste of that kingdom of God and are truly a witness of it. It is because of this that our fraternity is not simply a means by which to support the work of brothers, a utilitarian structure that offers support and encouragement so that we can go announce the kingdom. No, the fraternity is itself the announcement of the kingdom.

That is the life I seek. *That* is how I answer the ever-important questions of life: I will love and be loved by God and the brotherhood of men seeking to announce that kingdom by their lives, and that gives my life all the meaning I could ever want.

And yet, for some reason it is still not convincing enough for some people. For some reason, many cannot understand that I have chosen not to find a soul mate, not because I am not allowed or am unable, but because I have found another option that means more to me than that. I am not choosing a life without love or sacrificing what I truly want so that I can do something noble; what I want more than anything is a life of love, and I have found it here with the friars. Unfortunately, it does not stop people from asking this very sad, absolutely offensive question:

What If I Fall in Love?

"So, what if you take solemn vows, and after that, you meet a girl that knocks you off your feet and you fall totally in love? What do you do then? Are you allowed to leave?"

In the six months that I've been a postulant, and the two years I discerned religious life prior to entering, I heard this question too many times. Honestly, it's a truly despicable question. I find it to be very indicative of the culture from which it comes: one that is afraid of commitment and is obviously skeptical of celibate chastity, whether it's implicitly or explicitly realized.

For starters, it implicitly treats the choice to enter religious life as a "Plan B." If there is a possibility that someone would leave religious life for marriage (which there has to be in the mind of the questioner otherwise it would have never been asked), it means that God is not ultimately the first choice; religious life was an option chosen in the absence of one's soul mate, but if and when that person is found there is a new best option. In a surprisingly high number of cases, people who ask this question assume that the only reason people enter religious life is because they are either asexual or were incapable of forming and maintaining an intimate relationship with another.

The truth is, a large number of healthy men and women in religious orders have had experience in love (and yes, even sex) before entering and taking vows. In my own life before I decided to enter, I had experienced two, two-year-long relationships with women that I loved enough to marry and was fully aware of the prospect of finding another. My choice to be a part of religious life was not without other options, nor will it be without new options in the future. (Many will tell you it's not a matter of what to do "if" you fall in love, but rather "when.") Like all healthy religious, however, I discerned that my life would be more greatly fulfilled in celibate chastity than in marriage, and so it was my "Plan A" to seek God in this way.

I imagine that God is insulted by this question for the same reason: Is it not possible that someone could see a life fully devoted to God as the best option, an option greater than even the man/woman of one's dreams? Not only do I know that this is entirely possible, I feel very strongly that God has called me and others to this life, and that it is just as much his choice as it is ours. When I'm asked about leaving after solemn profession for the sake of "love," I get the sense that the asker either refuses to believe or is unable to understand that one can want a relationship with God in the form of a celibate chastity more than an exclusive relationship with another person.

The final, and most disappointing part of this question is that it completely disregards the gravity and sanctity of a covenant with God. Does solemn profession mean so little that one would be curious enough to ask whether or not a religious is willing to break it? I imagine that these same people wouldn't ask an engaged man, "So what happens if after you're married you meet a woman that knocks you off your feet and you fall totally in love? What do you do? Are you allowed to leave?" It's an incredibly insulting question. Why doesn't it sound as insulting when someone asks it about a commitment to religious life? Again, I think the person that asks this question implicitly values a commitment to God and an ascetic life less than a commitment to another person.

If you've asked this question before in your life, I forgive you. I imagine that the implications of the question were not quite realized at the time, and had you known, you would have never asked it. For others, I hope that it is just as appalling to you as it is to me, and you will help to create a culture that views a solemn commitment to God as an extraordinarily fulfilling way of life.

At this point, I'm a long way from professing any sort of formal vows, and so am quite free to leave whenever I wish. At the same time, I have placed the prospect of marriage on hold for a while as to enter into an intimate, exclusive relationship with God, discerning a lifelong commitment by essentially "dating God" (a term Dan Horan, OFM, has famously used.) If and when that day comes when I'm ready for solemn profession, and someone very unfortunately asks me what I would do if I fall in love, I'll have the perfect answer for them: "I already have."

That post, written at the beginning of my journey of religious life, is just as true today as I approach solemn vows. Even after receiving the habit, taking temporary vows, and lasting five years in this life, I still receive this question and struggle to answer it with charity. My conviction for this life has not changed and my disgust for the question has not waned.

But something has changed. Whereas the initial post was written from afar and in response to a hypothetical question, now, as I reflect back on the topic, I can answer from a position of experience. In my life as a friar, I *have* fallen in love with someone in a romantic way.

And when I did, I fell hard.

Prior to our first encounter, I believe I had gone more than five years as a friar barely finding another person attractive, let alone someone to fall in love with. I was so comfortable in my commitment to celibacy, thinking that there was likely no woman out there that could even amaze me at this point, that I barely thought about any other options when petitioning for permission to make my solemn vows. The question of marriage, I thought, had been so long ago answered that my being a friar for life was a forgone conclusion. Prior to our first encounter, I was living this life based on a decision I had made in 2010 to break up with my girlfriend and join the friars.

After our first encounter, I was a mess. I had forgotten what it felt like to fall that hard. Decompressing with a friend of mine—a man deeply in love himself and taking his marriage very seriously—he did not believe me at first. Surely it was just an infatuation. Surely it was just superficial. The more he pushed me, the more he asked about how I was feeling, the more it was clear to both of us: This was different than what I had said no to seven years earlier. Not only did I want to be with her, I found myself thinking about where she was from, what her hobbies were, and what she wanted to do with her life—three things that I had either no interest in or a strong feeling of discomfort about—and had no trouble picturing myself adopting all three as my own. The more I saw her, the deeper it got. As unbelievable and clichéd as it sounds, I found in her everything that I had always looked for in a girlfriend and struggled to find a flaw I could not easily overlook, if she had any at all. In an unfortunate moment of embracing the overly romantic, saccharine values of our time, I heard myself say deep within, "This is *the one* I am supposed to marry."

So, what happens if I fall in love? A number of things: I become incredibly distracted and unproductive for about a month as I struggle to deal with long-forgotten feelings; I experience tremendous turmoil and heartbreak that leaves me downright sick at times; and I suck it up and continue to go about my life as a Franciscan friar. Truly, that is what happened when I fell in love last year, and it will be what I do when I fall in love again. As tremendous as this woman is and as happy as I could have been spending my life with her, she— or any woman for that matter—is not what I want most in life. She is not the answer to my most important question. Finding one's soul mate, having kids, raising a family, and growing old together is a wonderful life. Many people embrace this life, and the Church needs more faithful examples of this. But not from me. As much as I would *love* to have such an amazing romantic companion as her—and all that goes along with it—I truly *love* being with the brothers in this life of penance and evangelization.

Is it without its drawbacks? Of course not. Do I desire, sometimes, the comfort of a soul mate? Absolutely. With every decision comes the knowledge that we have said no to everything else, that we cannot have everything in life. Sometimes, like meeting this woman or seeing such happy couples all around you, it can be difficult to see what we have said no to. But sometimes, it is in those moments that we can also be truly grateful for the path we have been called to follow. As I wrote at the start of 2017, spending time with my college friends and seeing their lives progress was bittersweet, but it also helped me keep my own life in perspective.

On My Own

For the past four years, I've spent New Year's Eve renting a house with friends I met freshman year of college. For two, sometimes three nights, we catch up, play games, and just enjoy the company of people we have known for nearly a decade, reminiscing about old times as we make stories worth telling next year. Now nine years removed from the time we all met living in the same freshman dormitory, twelve different people have attended at least one weekend and seven of us have attended them all. To say that it's one of my favorite times of the year is an understatement.

As the years roll on, so do our lives, and it's amazing to watch my friends grow up, to see their careers take off, and most significantly, to be a part of their lives as their personal relationships become more serious. While we have always included new boyfriends/girlfriends into the fold and "couples" have generally made up more than half of the group, this year marked a distinct step. Of the thirteen people attending, ten were with someone with whom they have been dating for more than three years (with the longterm boyfriend of another unable to attend and the other having just ended a serious two-year relationship with a former attendee), two sets of couples had gotten a pet together in the past year (and brought it with them), and one couple had even gotten married since last year.

And then there was me. Not in a relationship, not looking to be in one. While my friends are all really mature when it comes to the setting and are in no way exclusive or publicly affectionate while in the group, the gravity of the situation was impossible to miss: When each night was over and people went to bed, when we said our goodbyes and went our separate ways, everyone else had a partner. Everyone else had someone on the journey, someone to share a conversation with, to share their lives with.

Me? I had the radio. And it was a jerk.

"An' here I go again on my own

Goin' down the only road I've ever known,

Like a drifter I was born to walk alone."

With my friends on my mind, the first song I heard on the radio driving home was "Here I Go," by Whitesnake. Yeah... I didn't listen to the rest of the song.

But it got me thinking. As I continue to discern my life with the friars and my imminent decision of whether or not to make final vows in August, am I really choosing a life "on my own"?

The immediate and obvious answer is no. As I shared during my first year and have reiterated numerous times since, just because I am choosing to remain unmarried does not mean that I am choosing to forgo intimacy. There are multiple ways to love and be loved and I'm simply saying no to one of them. There is still the intimacy of platonic friends supporting each other through struggles, of work colleagues pouring their lives into a project, of academics challenging one another intellectually, of "the guys" working out and playing sports together, and of course, of the brothers in the fraternity committing their lives to one another, among many more. As a friar, I have and will continue to experience intimacy on many levels, feeling a part of something greater than myself, finding a permanent home with men who welcome unconditionally, and sharing in a common vision of life and Church. In a very true and important sense, I will never, ever be alone because I have the brothers.

And yet, five and a half years with the friars has shown me that, no matter how significant and important it is, a fraternity most certainly is not an equivalent alternative to a spouse. While, yes, both are lifestyles of intimacy and commitment, both are intended to be unconditional and lifelong, and both offer stability and produce fruit for the Church and world, they are fundamentally different in focus and lived experience: A marriage is based on a one-to-one, finely-chosen relationship while a fraternity consists of hundreds of unchosen ones. As similar as they may seem and as fruitful as both can be, choosing to love and making a commitment to one romantic partner will never, ever be the same as growing in and learning how to love a group of diverse, transient people. Like a married couple, I can say without question that in times of crisis and times of joy the fraternity will be there to share in and support me, but I cannot say with certainty who the individual men will be, where they'll be when I need them, or when I will see those most important to me. Very much unlike marriage, my decision to stay or leave the fraternity is not dependent on the individual members of it, and in fact, some of my closest friends within the fraternity have left the order, will eventually leave, or will ultimately die within my lifetime. Thus, even though many intimate relationships exist, my life within the fraternity will always have a sense of being "on my own."

Is this some unforeseen revelation that I've just now had? Am I beginning to question my life as a friar or fear what might be ahead? No. Not at all. As much as we can equate this life to being married or "having a new family," I knew even before I joined that these things were meant analogically. Similar, but not the same. Fraternal life can never fully replace true family life; fraternal intimacy is simply not the same as exclusive one-to-one intimacy.

But here's the thing: It doesn't need to be. As I grow in my life as a friar and prepare for my final vows, it's even more obvious to me that some people are simply not called to such an intense, one-to-one relationship, that, even though such relationships are the norm in most cultures, they are not necessarily the best way to love or build communities. Maybe some people, not for lack of love or ability but because of an abundance of both, are called and gifted in such a way to love whomever they are with, living intensely in the present moment without the long-term commitment of the future; maybe some people can live anywhere with anyone doing anything because their lives are not defined by the intense love they find and share in one person, but rather by the desire to be in relationship with the source of love itself and to share it in a broad sense with all.

Are these people—am I—"on [their] own"? In a sense, yes: They will never have the unconditional one companion with whom to share all their thoughts, fears, desires, and struggles. And maybe they can't live without that. But in another sense, no: They will always be guided by the One who loved first, both in their relationship to that love and in making it present in the world. And maybe I can't live without *that*.

As I mentioned in the opening chapter, discernment is rarely a decision between one ultimately good option and an infinite number of bad ones. Rather, we see before us multiple good pathways to God, pathways that will bring us joy and fulfillment, that will allow us to live our true calling as disciples in Christ. In my life, becoming a Franciscan friar and getting married were both amazing, possible ways to live out my vocation.

In my initial discernment, I, like many others, saw a life of celibate chastity in a fraternity with others to be one of great sacrifice: If I join the friars, I thought, then I cannot get married. I was worried about being lonely, about losing the assured sense of love that a lifelong companion offered. I was afraid of being "on my own," as it were.

After six years of living this life, I have found that no longer scares me. Maybe it is because I have found that the brothers—in all the ways they inspire me and in all they do to challenge me—are all the love and support I will ever need. Maybe it is because I have simply grown in maturity, and as I have become more confident in myself I realize that I do not need to rely on others as much. Or maybe, just maybe, it is because the subtle reminder that I do not have someone to call my own—that I am "on my own" without a soul mate— provides just enough insecurity in my life to realize that I truly need God above all else. Unable to rely solely on someone else for all the intimacy I need, I am forced to answer the two most important questions of adult life in the only way that makes sense to me: *Jesus* is the reason that my life has meaning, and *Jesus* is the one who will love me.

chapter **four**

Seeking Insecurity

Of all the many artistic depictions of St. Francis found around the world, my favorite cannot be found in a Church or museum, is not the centuries-old work of a renowned artist, and does not attract thousands of pilgrims a year. In fact, thousands of people probably *do* see it every day but do not even notice. On its own, it is but a simple, rather ordinary work of art—just a poor friar surrounded by a halo of gold doves begging for food and seemingly looking up to the sky. What makes this piece so extraordinary is not so much its artistic qualities as it is its location. A relief in the facade of a Manhattan department store, St. Francis permanently sits in the shadow of two of New York's most famous and formidable buildings: In front of him—the actual object of his upward gaze—is Rockefeller Center, a symbol of tremendous wealth and power in the secular world; behind him—presumably from where he has just come—is St. Patrick's Cathedral, a symbol of the tremendous wealth and power of the religious world. And there the poor beggar sits sharing his meal with a bird. Although neither condemning nor protesting either institution in any explicit sense, the humble saint's life serves as a radical juxtaposition and critique of the values of the world. He is not concerned with power. He is not interested in wealth. All he wants, with all his heart, is to be a poor imitator of Christ.

Our world, as St. Francis knew, values individual greatness. In order for our lives to be significant—in order to be "great"—we are told that we must obtain as much power, wealth, and prestige as we can, living in constant competition with one another to see who has the most and thus is the *best*. Our worth is defined by what we possess as it relates to what others possess, and those who have more than others live believing that they are owed certain things from the world. Respect. Admiration. Glory. Fear. Love.

This is not the Gospel of Jesus Christ that St. Francis lived by.

Against the values of the world, Jesus gave up his power in heaven to live as a poor outcast on earth. Although the king of the universe, he did not live or rule like the kings of earth: Loving his people as a shepherd loves his sheep, he led with mercy over judgment, justice over greed, reconciliation over exclusion, and humble service over heavy demands. He associated with the weak and the lowly while criticizing the rich and haughty, announcing a kingdom turned upside down in which the last shall be first and the first shall be last. To enter this kingdom, he told his followers to deny themselves, sell all they had, and take up their crosses daily in order to follow him. In his final act of humility—even though he was God and capable of all things—he willingly laid down his life so that others might live, telling his disciples that they were to do the same. Against the values of the world, Jesus Christ came preaching and *showing* that greatness is not found in power, wealth, and prestige, but rather in weakness, poverty, and humble service to the lost and forgotten.

What strange values, we might say. What *challenging* values.

And yet, these are not only the values of a thirteenth-century saint who lived an extraordinary life; these are the values that define our lives today as Christians. While St. Francis took the imitation of Christ as far as I believe it can go and made it easy for us to place him far from our reach on a pedestal, I am not convinced that the call to live a radical life of greatness as Jesus showed us is a particularly *Franciscan* charism. *All* of us are called to renounce our power, wealth, and prestige for the sake of the kingdom. *All* of us are called to put on weakness, poverty, and humble service to the lost and forgotten. The way I live as a Franciscan may be different in in style and emphasis, but the essence and inspiration are the same: A Franciscan life is simply a concerted effort to humbly live the Gospel, something that all Christians are called to do.

This post, written in my third year with the friars, was my attempt to "sell" the concept of Gospel poverty to those who felt it was the sole responsibility of the Franciscans.

Why Poverty?

Given that it is pretty much the antithesis of what most in the modern western world would consider to be a worthwhile life pursuit, it's a fair question. Why would one want to spend his or her life trying to be poor? I believe that there are at least four reasons for each and every Christian to consider.

1. Jesus was poor. Every year as we prepare for Christmas in the season of Advent, we recall that Jesus became flesh not in a castle but in a dirty manger; we recall that the first people to visit him were the shepherds, the ritually and materially "unclean" outcasts of society. Jesus coming in this way is an example of how he "emptied himself, taking the form of a slave." As Christians, those who follow Christ, we wish to be like Jesus by imitating his simplicity and humility; as Franciscans, those who follow Christ in a very literal sense, we wish to be like Jesus by imitating his material situation as well.

2. Jesus called his followers to be poor, for the poor. That being said, there are a number of things that Jesus did that we're probably not all called to imitate, dying on a cross, for example. Because of that, we must look to his words and exhortations. When Jesus called his disciples to follow him, "They left everything and followed him" (Luke 5:11, 5:28, 12:33, 14:33, 18:22; Mark 1:16-20; Matthew 4:18-22). Leaving their nets, money, family ties, prestige, and occupations behind, the disciples became poor in order to follow him. When he sent them out, he told them to go without walking stick, sack, food, money, or second tunic (Luke 9:2, Matthew 10:9; Mark 6:8).

And what did he preach to the people? "Blessed are you who are poor, for the kingdom of God is yours" (Luke 6:20). Given the pharisaical climate of observation of the purity laws in the Torah, it would have been revolutionary enough to say that the poor were more than worthless afterthoughts of God. To say that they were blessed, that there was something particularly special about their situation, was something so cataclysmic to our fallen nature that I believe it has yet to be fully realized in the Church. The poor are special, not in their relation to our charity, but in the very fact that they are poor.

3. We seek justice against a corrupt system. Because of that, there is an important distinction that needs to be made in order for us to live Gospel poverty appropriately and to relate to the poor compassionately: poverty that promotes virtue, which should be imitated, and poverty that demoralizes and dehumanizes, which should be eradicated. An excellent reason to remain poor is to take a stance against unjust systems that do not allow authentic human development and to stand in solidarity with those affected.

What sorts of stances does this entail? According to the United States Conference of Catholic Bishops in their 1986 letter, *Economic Justice for All,* this includes anything and everything that could adversely affect the poor:

> Decisions must be judged in light of what they do for the poor, what they do to the poor, and what they enable the poor to do for themselves. The fundamental moral criterion for all economic decisions, policies, and institutions is this: They must be at the service of all people, especially the poor. (no. 24)

The way we eat, save, spend, vote, travel, reside, and shop all have an impact on the poor. Do we ever stop to wonder how the way we live is possible? How else could our t-shirts be so cheap if it weren't for child labor? How else could our fast food be so cheap if it weren't for dehumanizing wages? The list goes on and on. Unless we curve our insatiable need for "stuff" and change our lifestyle, these atrocities will continue to happen to the poorest in society.

As St. John Chrysostom writes, "Not to share one's wealth with the poor is to steal from them and to take away their liveli-hood. It is not our own goods which we hold, but theirs." I believe very strongly that the extra coat one has in one's closet belongs to the poor; to keep it unused in one's closet rather than giving it to the poor is a grave sin.

So pervasive are these issues that they in fact take on a struc-tural nature. As Pope Francis writes in his latest apostolic exhor-tation *Evangelii Gaudium,* reiterating years of papal teaching, these structures need to be challenged:

Some continue to defend trickle-down theories which assume that economic growth, encouraged by a free market, will inevitably succeed in bringing about greater justice and inclusiveness in the world. This opinion, which has never been supported by the facts, expresses a crude and naïve trust in the goodness of those wielding economic power and in the sacralized workings of the economic system. (54)

4. Wealth too easily becomes a false god. Which brings us to the fourth and final reason to live a life of poverty: You cannot serve both God and mammon. The reason that our economic system in the west is so detrimental to the poor is because it has replaced God with money, a transition that is easy to make and difficult to break.

On the one hand there are those who have made it their life's pursuit to acquire money, equating wealth with happiness. This is a sad state of affairs. Many people fail to recognize that money cannot satisfy such an insatiable appetite, leading some to resort to morally reprehensible things to obtain or maintain wealth.

The answer, however, is not to become a miser, refusing to spend one's money on anything. Ironically enough, this is also a form of idolatry because it takes an exorbitant amount of time and energy away from things that actually matter.

* * *

It is because of all of this that I choose a life of poverty. I choose to imitate Jesus as closely as I can; to obey his word; to reject any system that may inhibit the authentic human development of my brothers and sisters; and to do all that I can to keep the Trinitarian God as my one and true God. I choose to live a life that is simple, without the distractions of useless possessions and futile pursuits. I choose to live a life that focuses entirely on a life with Jesus. That is why I choose to live a life of poverty.

When young St. Francis was first converted in mind and heart to leave his old world of vanity behind and to take up a life of religion, he did not know, at first, what to do. Knowing only that he had lived a life of such excess to that point, and seeing the unfulfilling desire for prosperity all around him—being that he was a merchant's son—the first thing that he did was to rid himself of all the material pleasures of life that weighed him down. He set off for a neighboring town with a horse and his expensive clothing, and upon arriving, he sold them all for a fair price. Not wanting to be burdened by the money he received, he stopped at a small church that had fallen into ruin, gave it all to the priest, and begged that he be able to stay in the church. Without anything of his own, he thought, he could begin his life as a follower of Jesus.

For me, the conversion of life was a little less dramatic but the desire was similar: To follow Jesus with my whole heart, I wanted to be unencumbered, and so before entering the friars and throughout my first two years, I tried to rid myself of anything that was not entirely necessarily. I gave away many of my books, kept only clothing that I wore on a regular basis, and left behind all of my games, hobbies, and extracurricular possessions. Looking around my room after moving in, I found immense comfort in the stark walls and empty closet. For me, like St. Francis after his conversion, there was absolutely no denying that material poverty was a major topic for Jesus. More than sexuality and marriage, ritual and religious laws, or peace and violence, Jesus spent his time with the poor, lived the life of poverty, and called his disciples to renounce what they have. With that much attention, I wanted to take it very seriously.

And yet, if the Franciscans have learned anything after eight hundred years of struggling to live up to this identity and fighting with one another over the right definition of what Gospel poverty actually looks like, it is that defining one's life solely on the word *poverty* is likely a dead end. A loaded and charged word that means different things to different people, using it as a measure for one's life in Christ is not only practically difficult to define, it misses the overall point of the Gospel: Poverty is not an end in itself—it is not the object of our worship—but a *means* to that which is greater. If poverty was the goal unto itself, perfect discipleship would always end in destitution and starvation. That is how one "wins" poverty. Surely, that is not what Jesus meant when he said blessed are the poor. Rather, poverty helps us get to Jesus and be in communion with those whom he deemed important, and so it should be taken seriously, but it is ultimately *Jesus* who we seek and *the poor* that we need to be with.

Poverty can never be our goal as Christians, and it can never be our only guide.

As we Franciscans have returned to our foundational sources since the Second Vatican Council and have come to a more complete understanding of the life and thought of our Father Francis than we ever had in our history, we see that he knew this all along. Even though he lived an extremely austere lifestyle and placed heavy burdens of fasting and deprivation on himself, what emerges from his *Admonitions* and final *Testament* of life is not a desire to be poor above all else, but to be completely and utterly reliant on the love and mercy of God. When he exhorted the brothers, he obviously wanted the brothers to be poor, but even poverty was at the service of a more important virtue: humility. Servants of God and man, imitating Jesus who humbled himself to be among us, they were to live as they were aptly called, the "lesser brothers."

In my opinion, this is where the true charism of the Franciscans finds its home and the model that we can offer for all Christians wanting to live as Jesus called us. Coming to this realization after my novitiate year in 2013, a year in which the topic of poverty was largely frustrating and misunderstood, I tried to put aside that word for a while and get to the heart of what Jesus was really asking us to do and what Francis truly lived: dependence on God.

Seeking Insecurity

Poverty as a virtue is a difficult concept to define, and an even more difficult concept to get a group of friars to agree on. My concept of poverty is different from Br. X's whose concept of poverty is different from Br. Y's. Do we imitate the poor, or do we attempt to eradicate poverty? Is the cheapest option the best, or should we seek the longer lasting and human-conscious options that are more expensive? I present these conflicts not to trivialize or relativize the issue but to point out that "poverty" as a goal is very vague, is difficult to define, and is easily spiritualized until actions are no longer virtuous at all. In order to remain faithful to the Gospel and the spirit of St. Francis, I think that additional language is necessary to focus our efforts.

One of these words that I have written about before is sufficiency. Over the past year, this has been a much more helpful word in terms of evaluating my life as a friar than the word poverty. "Do I have more than I need?" is a much easier question to answer than "Is this keeping with poverty?" Asking myself this on a regular basis has helped me to live more simply, and to remove any and all things from my life that I do not need.

But with my reflections around *kenosis* throughout this past year, I found that an ethic of sufficiency needs additional direction in order to live a Gospel life. To be sufficient is by definition to have enough. To have this as a goal, while it does limit the possibility of living with excess, is to also never experience deprivation of any kind, to never feel worry or doubt about one's livelihood, and to never relate to those who do not have enough. On it's own, it can allow us to be too safe. Even if we live within our means and without extravagance, when we have "enough," especially when "enough" is accompanied by security and predictability, we are allowed to live a life that is comfortable, and worst of all, complacent. When this happens, we begin to fail Gospel poverty and our communities will inevitably fail with it. With high security and predictability, there is no room for trusting God or looking to God to provide because we become the rulers and suppliers of our own well-being; there is no need for a sense of urgency in our work or in our communities because the status quo does not bother us; there is no opportunity for solidarity with the poor (or even with the middle class) because we can no longer relate to the anxiety of not being able to make ends meet.

Our natural response, however, is to do the complete opposite. Not only do we not seek the fruits of insecurity, we do everything in our power to rid every ounce of danger from our lives, often going to great lengths to acquire it: We work too much, we attack others as a way to defend ourselves, and we store up treasures that cannot save. We believe that our youth, skills, health, possessions, and social bonds will last forever, that they will keep us happy and safe from all harm. This is a facade. It is the acceptance of the lie that the gift is more important than the One who gives that gift. It is the acceptance of the lie that we are capable of controlling our own fate, that all that we have acquired is somehow our own to possess, and that we received it based on our own merit. It is the acceptance of the lie that we are our own saviors.

So what does "seeking insecurity" look like? First of all, it does not look like being irresponsible, frivolous, or lazy. When we seek insecurity, we're not making bad decisions to squander away the gifts we've been given. We do not strengthen our relationship with the Giver by misusing his gifts. The real virtue lies in simply accepting that insecurity is all around us. When we accept the poverty that we have absolutely no control over our fate, that all we have is freely given, unmerited favor from God, we begin to relate to our possessions, to others, and to God in a completely different way. With this realization, all is gift, and God is the only one worth relying on. In times of great favor, we give glory to God; in times of trouble, God is the first we seek for help; at all times, we are unwilling to waste our lives acquiring, maintaining, and protecting possessions that fade at the expense of relationships that last.

Obviously, there are just as many holes in this ethic as there are with an ethic of sufficiency, but I think together they offer greater grounding in Gospel poverty than "poverty" alone. They force us to look at the issue outside of dollars and cents alone, and focus the discussion on the purpose for the virtue in the first place: Relationship with God. In the end, I think that we are only truly free when we accept that we are not in control and choose to seek the One who is. That's true insecurity worth seeking.

For the first two years of formation with the friars, with the goal of "poverty" on my mind, I debated quite a bit with myself about what I should do with the leftover stipend money I had each month. Not needing anything in particular at the time but knowing that I would one day have some costly needs, I debated: Should I return the money to the house and request money whenever I needed new shoes, computer, jacket, or should I hold onto that money, frugally saving it so that I could purchase those things on my own when necessary? At first, I chose the latter. I did not like the idea that I could simply go to the guardian or treasurer of the house whenever I needed something and it would magically appear. That is not the way it works for the poor; if they need something expensive, they either save until they have enough or take on debt that takes time and sacrifice to pay off. That—an imitation of the poor—was what I thought was best.

What I found, however, was that imitating the poor, or trying to be poor just for the sake of being poor, missed the point of what Jesus was saying and actually made me a lot *less* poor in spirit. You see, after just a few months, I had control over a decent amount of money that I had saved. And even though it was technically *my* money that I had not spent from previous months, the ever-increasing reserve of money left me much more independent, self-sufficient, and with greater purchasing power than I had before. I did not need anyone else's help or permission to buy something, I could do it myself. I was all that I needed. While we are talking very small sums of money here and I would have obviously needed permission and help to buy anything substantial, the negative effect is clear: As my own sufficiency and security rose, my dependence on others dropped.

This, I believe, is at the heart of Jesus's call to renounce the wealth we possess; this is why he tells us that it is easier for a camel to enter through the eye of a needle than someone who is rich to enter heaven. Is there something inherently wrong with being rich? Based on other stories, I would say no. Zacchaeus only gave up *half* of what he owned. *Someone* was feeding and housing Jesus and the disciples when they traveled. Even the woman who possessed the expensive perfumed oil used to anoint Jesus was *applauded* for giving him such a luxury rather than using it for the poor. The problem is not that wealth is inherently bad, it is that wealth often serves as a stumbling block to completely trusting in God. The fact that the rich young man of Matthew's Gospel had a lot of wealth is not the problem: It is that he treasured and *relied on* his wealth more than he did the Father, so much so that he was unwilling to give it up to follow Jesus. His wealth was more than just a possession to him; it had become a false god preventing him from seeking what was truly important.

The reason we can say poverty is a virtue is because it eliminates the ability for us to be self-sufficient and instead forces us to rely solely on God. Quite contrary to the common adage that says "God helps those who help themselves," we see throughout the Bible and human history the exact opposite: God is constantly going to the poor, the weak, and the helpless *precisely because they cannot help themselves.* Not the rich. Not the haughty. No, they do not need God. I think about my own life: When things are going well and I have everything I need, I rarely think to spend hours in prayer petitioning for God's grace; but throw in some distressing situations and take away my ability to fix my own problems and see how quickly I run to God. When we as Christians seek to be poor as Jesus taught us, we do so not for its own sake and not because dehumanizing conditions are virtuous, but because it strips away our temptation to be our own saviors and instead points us to the only one who can save us.

That is the Gospel poverty St. Francis lived.

With this now as our guide, it is easy to see that "poverty" as a virtue means much more than just the lack of wealth; Gospel poverty, as Jesus called us to be and to live, is a state in which we are stripped of all that prevents us from following him with complete abandon and without counting the cost. *Anything* that we have that lets us believe we can make it on our own and do not need God needs to be renounced. As Jesus tells us, "If your right hand causes you to sin, cut it off and throw it away."

What do we possess in our lives that needs to be cut off and thrown away?

When I looked at my life during novitiate and evaluated everything I possessed—not just the physical possessions but everything that I could claim as my own—I saw that I was privileged with so much in my life that I had begun to count as my own and take for granted. More than just wealth, I realized that there were many things in my life that I treasured very much and was forced to wonder if I had become like the rich young man: Could I give *that* part of me up to follow Jesus?

This post, reflecting on Jesus's self-emptying in the Letter to the Philippians, inspired me to look beyond the basic definitions of being materially poor and pushed me toward completely emptying myself before God.

Kenosis: What Could I Let Go of?

At the beginning of the year I was moved by Jesus's Kenosis, his self-emptying of his divine privilege, to become human:

"Though he was in the form of God,
[Jesus] did not regard equality with God
something to be grasped.
Rather, he emptied himself,
taking the form of a slave,
coming in human likeness;
and found human in appearance,
he humbled himself,
becoming obedient to death,
even death on a cross." (Philippians 2:6–8)

Jesus, the second person of the Triune God, chose to empty himself of his power, his will, his security, his appearance, and his life, in order to take on our humanity. What an act of humility! Rather than being called king and worshipped by angels, he was born into poverty, disrespected by many, and executed an innocent man. What an act of trust! Instead of being able to rely on his own authority or ability, Jesus left himself at the mercy of his Father, and remained obedient to the end. What an act of love! John tells us, "God so loved the world that he gave his only Son."

Jesus's self-emptying is the perfect act that Francis spent his entire life attempting to imitate. It is the reason that our Order is called the Order of "Friars Minor," literally the "lesser brothers," and why poverty is so crucial to our charism. Our lives are an act of emptying anything and everything that could leave us feeling self-reliant, in control of our own fate, proud, or above others, in order that we may be totally reliant on God's love and mercy.

Moved by this, I decided to make an inventory of absolutely everything I could claim as my own. If I were to follow the example of our Lord with my own act of kenosis, what would I need to give up in order to be completely reliant on God in humility, trust, and love?

At the top of the list were all of my possessions. These were the easiest to think of and included my laptop, camera, music, pictures, and clothes, among other things. I've reflected before on the need to keep possessions simple and to make sure that I use them in keeping with Gospel poverty, but now I wonder what it would be like to renounce ownership or use of everything. Luke's Gospel mentions a number of times that the disciples of Jesus "left everything and followed him." Could I do this?

As if that question isn't difficult enough to answer, the rest of the inventory only got harder as I went on. What about all of my legal assets? I have a driver's license, a decent credit score, US citizenship that includes a right to vote and protections under the law, and as a religious I am tax exempt. The list goes on. I have physical assets such as good health, all of my limbs, working senses, free of any malformations, and fit enough to perform all basic tasks on my own. I have intellectual assets such as normal memory skills, basic brain functioning, and an ability to study at a university. I have social assets that allow me to keep a desirable reputation, friendships, respect from peers and superiors, and the occasional praise. Lastly, I have assets related to the Church: Personally, I am in good standing, have a right to teach and preach, have the backing of an Order, and structurally the Church is alive, it is organized, and there are many opportunities to be active in it in this country.

So I ask myself: What if, like Jesus, I was an alien in a foreign land, was an innocent man treated as a criminal, or was an outcast in society? What if I were to contract a disease that left me physically or mentally dependent on others for basic tasks? What if my reputation was ruined, people no longer liked me, or I was left without any friends? What if the Church was to reject me, the Order was suppressed, or the Church structures were to crumble? Or what if, in a much more likely situation, I was given a direct order to do something without consulting my desires?

In moments of loss, whether it be life-changing or normal day-to-day disappointments, self-inflicted or imposed, there is the possibility for the greatest gain. In recognizing the futility of all of the many things we claim as our own and divesting ourselves of the ownership, feeling of entitlement, and need for any one of them over God's love, we become free. In these moments, we are being asked to focus less on the gift that has been taken away from us and more on the One who gave it in the first place, the One who wishes to give us even more in return. In times of self-emptying, we realize how futile it is to put our trust in money, good looks, education, or a host of other things that have meaning to us, things that do not last, and how even more ridiculous it is to fight endlessly to maintain control over them.

My goal in all of this is to free myself of any need to control, appropriate, defend with violence, or hoard any gift from God as if that gift were an end in itself. In making this inventory, I seek not to rid myself of all of God's many gifts, but to recognize the generous bounty of God in my life and to be more dependent on him.

The image I leave with is one that I recently heard in a homily. God's abundant generosity is like the air all around us. We are gifted freely with more life-giving air to breathe than we could ever consume, and yet, we have a tendency to hold onto this breath, to claim it as our own, and to be afraid to exhale. What good is that gift to us if we hold onto it? We will eventually suffocate, and the air will leave us whether we like it or not. What I've learned from Jesus's experience of kenosis is that it is only in the exhale, the letting go of all that we have, that we are ever able to receive anything else. It is in the letting go of all that we cling to, and the trust that God will provide for us just as he did before, that we are free to love and be loved by God.

Although St. Francis had taken a tremendous step toward perfect Gospel poverty in selling all that he had and living as a poor hermit in a dilapidated church, he still possessed so much in the world. With a wealthy merchant for a father and his mother desiring that he return to the comfort of the family home to one day be a successful merchant himself, he knew that he had not completely left the world. At any moment, he could leave the church and take up, once again, the lavish life he once knew. The more his father coerced him into returning, the more the safety net of his family and his family's wealth hung over his head. That too, he understood, he had to renounce. And so, in a dramatic act of kenosis in front of the bishop in the middle of the city, he stripped himself of the clothes he had received from his parents and in a powerfully symbolic gesture, handed them back as he announced that he had no father but the Father in heaven. From that day forward, he no longer claimed a right to the family name and all of the power, influence, safety, and comfort that it afforded him. Now, not only had he given up his wealth, he had given up his social status in society. For all intents and purposes, he was a nobody to society.

In my case, once again, the act of renunciation was a bit less dramatic and not quite as powerful, but important nonetheless. A month into our novitiate year, I took part in a ceremony with the other novices called "divestiture." Given a large envelope, we were told to place within it anything we felt would get in the way of actively entering into the year of prayer, fraternity, and conversion. I cannot remember everything I enclosed, but two things stick out in my mind as particularly significant. The first was the official notice I received when I closed my bank account weeks earlier. For me, the bank account was not just a place where I kept my few dollars, it symbolized my financial independence, the way I had taken care of myself and bought everything I wanted for more than ten years. Although we were not required to give it up, I found it to be a must in my life as a friar. I did not want to be independent or self-sufficient anymore. The second significant object that I can remember was a letter I had received from a fan of my blog during the previous year. In a simple sense, it was a reminder that I had been required to give up writing for a year while in the novitiate, and served as a sign of the vow of obedience I was about to take. On a deeper level, though, it represented all the favor and acclaim I loved to receive and secretly wanted more of. Living this life, I decided, was not about being popular or well-liked, and even though it is nice to be supported, my vocation was not to be influenced by or dependent on what others thought of me. Symbolically, I placed that letter into the envelope as a way of giving up that desire in myself and the benefits it afforded. I did not want that anymore.

Looking back years later, there is definitely a part of me that finds the ceremony a bit contrived and maybe even a little too sentimental; for many of us, there was almost no *actual* effect on our lives in renouncing what we did, and at the end of the year, most of us received back what we had given up. In that way, it was a nice but hollow ritual.

That notwithstanding, the sentiment behind the ritual is an essential part of our lives as Christians and is something that we should challenge ourselves to do on a regular basis. What do I possess in life? In what ways are these possessions gifts from God and in what ways are they sources of my own arrogance and privilege? Am I willing and able to give these things up to follow Jesus, and if not, why? Maybe we do not need to formalize these questions into a ritual, but as men and women who call ourselves followers of Jesus, there must be something in our lives driving us to imitate his kenosis in a real way, calling us to actively renounce that which gets in the way of being poor and humble, just as Jesus was. The kingdom of heaven, as taught to us by Jesus and lived out by St. Francis, is one of renouncing all that we have to embrace weakness, poverty, and humble service to the lost and forgotten. All of us are called to follow.

Unfortunately, this is not always possible.

As I continued to reflect on all the many privileges in my life over the next few years and began to work on my own life of kenosis, I came to a tragic conclusion in my fourth year with the friars that, not only might I not achieve the goal of perfect kenosis, I might not even come close. Quite obviously, there are some things that just *cannot* be renounced no matter how hard we try, and as much as I wanted to be a minor in society, I realized that there was almost nothing I could do to make that happen. I was, am, and always will be a part of the privileged in the world.

Not So Minor

A man of great conversion, Francis is probably most well-known for dramatically renouncing his earthly wealth and high social status in order to minister to the lepers, those people so sick and disgusting that they needed to live outside the city (and wear a bell so that people could run away when they heard them coming). The Franciscan charism follows in his example: As members of the Order of Friars Minor, the "lesser brothers," we are called to live a life for the poor, with the poor, as the poor, renouncing any sort of wealth, power, or status that would nurture a feeling of entitlement or honor. The lowest in society do not expect to be served or cared for; they know that they must serve others. That is what Francis wanted.

When I look at my own life, I struggle to identify a single way in which I am a minor in our society: I am a young, white, college-educated, middle class, heterosexual male, born in the United States to parents who are still married, a member of the largest religious organization in the world, and have no mental or physical disabilities. If that's not enough, I joined one of the largest religious orders in the Catholic Church, giving me tremendous (and largely undeserved) respect as a religious and future member of the clergy. In literally every way that I can imagine I find myself among the privileged in society.

And unlike Francis who was able to renounce his status in society with a symbolic undressing before the bishop, I can hardly renounce the attributes that make me privileged in this one.

As I see racial discrimination continue to boil over in places like Ferguson, Missouri, I am reminded that my race will never be a problem for me. Upon arriving in Camden, New Jersey, for a summer assignment, one friar told me, "Oh don't worry, you're white. The gang members and drug dealers won't hurt you because they don't want to scare away their white customers."

As I watch news coverage of the recent border crossings and immigration laws in Arizona and Georgia, I know that I will never be "randomly" stopped on the street and forced to prove that I belong, have to flee one country into a country that does not want me, or have to worry about my rights when abroad.

As a male, I know that I will never be given less money for doing the same job as a co-worker, fear being alone outside at night, or constantly have to prove myself and my gender as not inferior.

As our Church and country continues to understand homosexuality, I am made aware that I have never had to worry about how my sexuality or sexual orientation could offend someone, what people might think of me if they found out, or being thrown out of my house by my parents.

This list could go on and on. As I look out into the world, I see people being discriminated against and made "lesser" in our society each day, and it is never me. I doubt it ever will be. And so I'm faced with a challenge. How do I ever become "lesser" in society? How do I ever even approach minority when things like race, gender, sexual orientation, education, and physical capability are not exactly things that can be stripped and handed to a bishop?

It is here that I would normally have a conclusion like, "For me, what's important is... The key is... I've found that the best answer is..." Unfortunately, my reflection today is a little less complete than normal. The fact of the matter is that I simply do not know and I will have to sit with this struggle for a while longer. There are obviously some things that I can change: how I spend my money, with whom I associate, how intentional I am at being with the poor. As I leave formation and enter into a more autonomous life as a friar, I know that there will be a little more freedom to choose where and how I live, and what ministry I do, making this a little easier to live out.

And yet, there is a part of me that realizes that I will never be the least in society, and I am struggling to accept that. How can I say I want to be a friar minor, an imitator of Jesus and Francis of Assisi, with so much respect, authority, privilege, and "wealth," both civilly and ecclesiastically? I don't know. For now, all I can do is realize that this "great privilege" I have in our society is nothing but a lucky ticket in the womb lottery: I have done nothing to deserve it and ultimately am no better off than anyone else because of it. I am what I am before God, and nothing more. This is a bit of wisdom that I must always keep with me. For though I may never be able to fully renounce all that separates me from the least in our society, I know there is always a full reserve of pretension, entitlement, and arrogance just waiting to be given up inside me. If I want to be minor in society, it starts with the attitude I bring to every situation: I am here to serve the people of God with perfect humility and minority, and they do not owe me anything because it is God who is truly doing all the work.

As I have had time to think about this issue further in the last few years, and as the concept of inalienable privilege—particularly as it relates to race—has come to the fore in our public square since first writing this post, I think a more concrete response is necessary than I was able to give originally. What do we do with the privileges we cannot possibly renounce?

The first step to recovery, they say, is admitting that we have a problem. In this case, our problem is that our world does not value everyone equally and some of us have inherent and inalienable traits that are worth more to others. I am a straight, white, educated male, and I cannot change that. No matter what I do in life or where I go, I will always have this "currency" with me offering me special privileges that others are not afforded. Even last year when I found myself as the only white person in a small, poor town in Mexico, unable to speak the language and completely useless to others, I found people who looked like me on the television, I received special attention from restaurant staff, and beggars always came immediately to me. Now, I could sit back and deny that I have anything more than others, pretend that sexism, racism, homophobia, and elitism do not exist and that I am not the beneficiary of these things... or I could admit that there is a problem in our world that gives me undue privilege and others undue suffering. Although seemingly insignificant, publicly admitting that there is a problem and validating the experience of true minorities is a crucial step forward.

Once we have admitted that there is a problem, I think the next thing we have to do is go to the people who do *not* have such privileges and listen to them. What has their experience been like? What issues have true minorities been silently dealing with for years while the privileged were comfortable in their ignorance? For St. Francis, there was nothing more transformative in his life than when he went among the lepers, those who were the outcasts of society and deemed worthless, and cared for them. I can only imagine the stories he must have heard from them, how his worldview was completely changed when he no longer saw them as "other" but as his fellow brothers and sisters in Christ. My guess is that, even though he and his brothers did wonderful work in the leprosariums, it was the brothers who left more changed after their encounter than the lepers. So it is our call as Christians when we have been blessed with such privileges. We go among others not out of condescension or to teach them about us, but to discover the great gifts God has bestowed on them—and the horrible tragedies society has forced them to endure—that we have failed to notice before.

Once we have admitted that there is a problem and have humbled ourselves to be in relationship with those we once considered "other," the final step is to do everything we can to change the situation. As a professor of mine used to say, "Once you know, you've got to go." As men and women who have committed ourselves to following Jesus and imitating his kenotic poverty in this world, how could we go back to our place of privilege on high having learned what we have? We are called to go deeper—to go *out*—and eliminate from the world what does not hold to Gospel values.

This final reflection of this chapter, written after a viewing of the movie *El Norte* and a discussion with the friars during my fourth year, captures the great angst I felt when I found myself with my eyes opened to a world of injustice and called to do something about it.

Franciscan Justice: A Life of Minority

Filmed in English, Spanish, and Maya, the movie depicts the lives of two Guatemalan exiles that flee oppression and violence in their village for what they believe will be the answer to all of their problems: the north. After a dangerous journey through Mexico, they realize that their idealized view of the United States is but a fantasy. Despite the affluence around them, they are no better financially than they were before. Life is difficult.

What I found most tragic about this story (a story with no happy ending, I might add) is the monologue the woman gives on her deathbed. She says, "In our own land, we have no home. They want to kill us. In Mexico, there is only poverty. We can't make a home there either. And here in the north, we aren't accepted. When will we find a home, Enrique? Maybe when we die, we'll find a home."

Can there be anything more tragic? I think about all of the people who live this reality each and every day, forced to leave behind all that is familiar for a new language, new culture, new climate, new set of relationships, and a new way of life, and it breaks my heart to think about the level of dejection they must feel. They have no home. They are strangers, outcasts of society.

When I look at my own life through this lens, it devastates me. In a material sense, look at all I have. In contrast, the characters in this movie fantasized about having a house with a toilet. But it's much more than that. I can honestly say that the most dejected I have ever felt was in a language class. Here I was, a confident (even cocky), intelligent, comfortable guy reduced to speaking like an infant, unable to express myself, and feeling like an idiot because I couldn't catch on. My whole world was reduced to nothing in those moments. I felt trapped and helpless. That was for one hour a day and it could end up ruining the rest of the day sometimes. Can I even imagine what it must feel like to do that for twenty-four hours a day, away from friends and family all the while living in fear of being caught without documentation? Such a level of dejection and dehumanization I will never feel.

Which brings me to the JPIC reflection for the month: How can I actually be minor when I know that people live like this minutes from my house. As a Franciscan, we are called by our General Constitutions "to have the life and condition of the little ones in society, always living among them as minors. In this social environment they are to work for the coming of the Kingdom" (Article 66). How is this even possible? In a very real sense, the most devastating thing about this movie is that it forces me to look at my own life and to realize there is nothing "minor" about it. The material possessions at my disposal, the social connections to guide and support me, the legal status that I possess, and the comfort I have in feeling that I am "home" in my own culture and speaking my own language ensure that I will never be as minor as those I serve. There is something about being comfortable that can never be minor.

And so I reflect. I take this with me to prayer for the rest of the month (and undoubtedly longer) as I try to figure out how I can see to act justly in this world and to do so as a friar minor. Part of me knows that I will never come to the answer that is perfectly satisfying in every way, but that's okay. As a friar minor, I am called to a life of constant conversion, a life of asking these questions and evaluating my life so to actually be the person I say that I am.

Just as "poverty" is not the ultimate value to be sought on its own but rather a means to achieving something greater, so it is with striving for minority status and emptying ourselves of our privilege. What good is it to be in relationship with the poor and strive to be minors ourselves if these things do not lead to a radical transformation in the way we interact with the world? Jesus asks these of us, not for their own sake, but so we have what it takes to follow him on his mission. What matters above all is not what is necessary to follow him but the very mission itself. Once we have been shown the great power, wealth, and prestige that exists in our lives above and against our brothers and sisters, and once we have set it as our life's goal to empty ourselves so to live with weakness, poverty, and humble service to the lost and forgotten, we are not complete in our journey. No, it is at that point that we are finally able to *begin* the journey to what matters: *to join Jesus in building up the kingdom of God through justice.*

When Jesus came to earth to walk among us, he did not do so simply to experience what we experienced, to give us strength and encouragement to continue living how we were living, or to teach us nice things. Jesus came as the great prophet of the Father to stand against the values of our world and to announce the coming of the kingdom of heaven. In coming in poverty and serving his people rather than demanding their praise, he was not just being a nice guy or a wise teacher, he was making a powerful and controversial claim against the wealth and power of this world in order to lead his people to the true kingdom with the true king. All that he did and all that he gave up were meant to point to that reality and to call the world around him to live for the justice of the kingdom that awaited them. By calling his people to poverty and humility, what he was really doing was calling for a radically converted people, concerned with heavenly justice, to be his prophetic voice in the world.

It is with this that we can return to the powerful image of St. Francis in the relief of the department store and understand with greater fullness its prophetic value. At first glance, we can marvel at the austerity of his material poverty and admire his ability to live with so little. But that is not what made St. Francis so amazing. Looking a little deeper, we might find ourselves inspired by a man who gave up everything—not just wealth, but everything he could ever claim as his own—to follow Jesus without reservation. But that, still, does not capture all of who the little saint was. It is only when we take in the whole context of the piece, placing the subject between the buildings around him and all that they mean, that the completeness of his life comes to the fore: Having given up everything to follow Jesus, humbling himself to go among the least in society as a brother, he was able to announce the kingdom of heaven and radically stand against the values of his day. St. Francis was not concerned with power. He was not interested in wealth. All he wanted, with all his heart, was to be a poor imitator of Christ. In poverty. In humility. And in justice.

As Christians, that is our call. That is what the world needs from us.

· · · · · ·

chapter **five**

_____

What the World Needs

When I was a kid, one of the most popular books in the elementary school library was the illustrated *Guinness Book of World Records*. Page after page showed extraordinary feats more unbelievable—and bizarre—than the last. Most hamburgers eaten in three minutes. Fastest 100-meter dash on crutches. Largest distance covered riding a unicycle. Most concrete blocks broken while holding an egg. Fastest mile jumping on a pogo stick while juggling three balls. Whether it was the incredible amount of skill exhibited by one person or the very absurdity of the task that he or she had mastered, something about those books fascinated us kids beyond belief. These people had found what they were *going to do with their lives* and some might even say their "calling."

Interesting... Could "long-distance pogo stick juggling" really be a vocation?

Based on my own journey and the suggestions I offered in the opening chapter to help in the discernment process, it would be very easy to see how this could be the case. Knowing that following God is life-giving rather than oppressive, and that God gives us gifts so that we can use and share them rather than hide them, discerning two questions—*does this bring me joy?* and *what am I good at?*— can be incredibly helpful in guiding our path. If someone likes to jump on a pogo stick while juggling for long periods of time, and they are good at it, then maybe that is exactly what God wants them to do with their life.

But maybe not.

While a vocation does bring us joy and should be something that we are good at, it is not primarily concerned with either of these things. As the word indicates, a vocation—from the Latin *vocare*, "to call"—is something that comes from outside and for the sake of something other than ourselves. Against the values of the world that tell us to never do anything we do not like and to think of our own happiness first, someone with a vocation is concerned most with the needs of the *caller* rather than their own, willing to sacrifice their own immediate happiness and comfort for the sake of the call. For them, there is a mission much greater than themselves at stake and they are willing to do whatever it takes to fulfill it. Sometimes, this means accepting that what we want to do and what we are good at is not what the world needs.

This was absolutely the struggle of St. Francis early in his life.

As a young and charismatic man, living in the midst of a rising entrepreneurial world, he had his heart set on being a knight, fighting against the enemy and bringing glory to his city. After returning from an unfortunate failed first attempt at being a warrior, he had his first encounter with God in a dream. There, God showed him a house filled with the weapons and shields of a glorified knight and told little Francis that these belonged to him. Overjoyed, he interpreted this as a call to try again and immediately set off to join the Fourth Crusade.

While on the way, however, God appeared to St. Francis in another dream and asked him this question: "Who can do more for you, the servant or the Lord?" (2 Celano, 245) Knowing of course that it was better to serve the Lord than the servant, Francis understood at that moment that the battle he was called to fight was not for earthly kings but for the One who gave those kings their authority: The Lord. *God did not need another sword-carrying crusader. The world did not need more war.* What it needed was someone to put on the "armor of light" and lead his people in spiritual battle. When he awoke, he immediately set off for his return to Assisi, determined to be what God and the world needed.

A year later, after selling all that he had and taking refuge in the poor, dilapidated church of St. Damien, St. Francis had a second encounter. Gazing upon the cross, he heard these words: "Francis, don't you see that my house is being destroyed? Go, then, and rebuild it for me" (Legend of the Three Companions, 76). In that moment, the Lord spoke directly to him and called him on a mission. *Rebuild my church.* There it was, the command he had been waiting for, the direction he was seeking to find. So direct and tangible, he knew what he was supposed to do and he immediately went out to do it: Buying or working for materials, he began literally rebuilding the fallen structure around him, brick by brick.

Once again, although it was a noble cause that certainly made St. Francis feel productive at the time, he later came to understand these words very differently. As his encounter with the lepers began to sink in and his eyes were being opened wider each day to the life and mission of Jesus Christ, he came to realize that *God did not need another builder of inanimate stones. The world did not need more fancy churches.* Seeing the body of Christ suffering and excluded in the lepers, corrupted and misguided in the scandals of the institutional Church, and lost and forgotten in the ordinary people, he understood that the house that he was supposed to rebuild was not one made of rock and confined to one place but the one made up of of the whole body of Christ and found all around him.

Even though fighting against the enemy and rebuilding fallen church buildings might have brought St. Francis joy and fulfillment, and even though they would have been easier and more comforting than going among those whom he had utterly despised his whole life, he knew that his mission was greater than his immediate comfort or fulfillment. His call was to live for the sake of the world, building up the kingdom of God.

And so it is ours as well. The real question is, *what does that look like?*

Building off of what I suggested in the first chapter, namely, that our essential call is to be a disciple of Jesus Christ and that there are an infinite number of ways of doing that, I have no intention of offering specific tasks that each Christian should do or particular ministry efforts that are more important that others; such an exercise would only serve to unjustly limit the ever-growing ways to serve God in the modern world. Rather, in this chapter on mission, I would like to offer three essential and universal principles (along with one shameless Franciscan plug) for evaluating one's call and living for the sake of the kingdom, things that I believe the world desperately needs. So, could "long distance pogo stick juggling" really be a vocation? If it enables us to do these three things, it just might be.

This first reflection, written in 2015 shortly after my first day volunteering as a chaplain in a hospital, offers us a solid starting point for discipleship in Christ: We need to listen and see as God does before we can do anything for the world.

What a Dying Man Who Didn't Say a Word Taught Me

On my first day, I visited a patient that was very near to death. When I came to his room, he was unconscious, and his wife indicated that it would not be long before he was gone. It was obvious. In the bed before me was someone sick and weak, entirely dependent on the outside world to survive. There was very little to see in that bed.

And yet, there was something profound about the experience. In just the few seconds I spent in his room, I felt something come over me. I couldn't say exactly what I was feeling at the time, but when I looked at this tired old man, beyond the years of being respected and "useful," I thought about how he must have been at one point. Sure, he was a withered old man now, but wasn't he a child at one time, full of energy and optimism? Wasn't he a young man at one time, in love and eager to take on the world? Mustn't there have been a time in his life when he was so very sure of himself, capable to take on the day? There had to be more than this shell of a man I saw.

As it was a busy day of orientation, I didn't think much more of him until later that evening when another friar and I watched the movie *Wit*. A homework assignment for our ministry class, *Wit* is a movie about a renowned and confident professor who develops and eventually dies of cancer. Through the process of following this woman's struggle with aggressive, experimental treatment methods, the viewer comes to understand and know the great physical pain and emotional trauma one goes through in such a situation. Emma Thompson's performance was so raw and so technically precise that I wanted to look away at times... but I couldn't. Her portrayal was absolutely chilling. Award-worthy, if you ask me.

But it is not her pain that made this movie so relevant to my experience earlier in the day, it was her existential crisis. Through numerous flashback scenes and monologues, the viewer is made aware from the beginning that she is no ordinary woman. Not only a professor at a distinguished university, she is a renowned research scholar with countless publications and accolades. To say that she is brilliant does little to appropriately distinguish her from her inferior colleagues. From her perspective (and the perspective of the viewer), her identity is defined by her long life and many accomplishments; cancer was but a footnote to how she understood herself, an afterthought on an otherwise note-worthy life.

But this is not who she is in the hospital. To the medical personnel, her primary identity is as a cancer patient. As such, she is seen and treated like all of the other patients: with concern and dignity, but as an utterly sick and weak person, entirely dependent on the outside world to survive. Having no knowl-edge of her life prior to treating her, they do not glory in her bril-liance or fear her reputation; they simply see a bald-headed, toxin-ridden body that had little-to-no chance of survival. Given their perspective, and there's no way you could blame them for this, her identity is intrinsically linked to having cancer, and their association with her reflects this. It was as if her life began when she entered the hospital doors and her life was defined by who she was there.

On an existential level, this aspect of the movie tore me up. There she was throughout the movie, a woman filled with an entire world of unique memories, having lived through trials and fears, joys and despairs and eventually making a reputation of greatness and incredible self-worth for herself...completely unnoticed and treated like anyone else. No one, even the one who treated her nicely, saw her for who she was at her best. They saw her for who she was at her worst: a cancer patient. How painful this must have been emotionally. How lonely she must have felt. How insignificant her life seemed to become. The way she narrated and acted with those in the hospital all but cried out, "This is not who I am! Don't you know this? I've lived fifty years of greatness and all you see is me at my weakest, me at the end! This is not who I am!"

Isn't that so true? Who of us is at our strongest when we are at a hospital? Who of us is at our best when we are sick? One might say that it is exactly the opposite: To go to a hospital is to be at one's most vulnerable, to admit sickness, brokenness, and need for healing. We are hardly who we are at our weakest state.

It was with this that my experience from earlier in the day came flooding back to me. Like the professor in *Wit*, I thought about how emotionally painful it must have been to be in his situation. I thought about how embarrassing, even, it must be to be a grown man with seventy years of accomplishments and experiences and yet have people see him for only the person he was in the moment, the weak, helpless man on his deathbed. Everyone who casually walked in and out of his room saw one man, but is that really the man he thought himself to be? I hardly think so. How difficult it must be to be faced with such an existential crisis at such a weak time. "Doesn't anyone know the real me?"

I can hardly fault the doctors or nurses for how he must have felt as their preoccupation is clearly on medical issues. One could even argue that they are simply not trained to deal with such issues. In fact, I'm not sure if I would want my doctor to know the deepest desires of my soul. But in that situation, I would definitely want someone to know. And so many do. In situations like these, so many people just want someone to talk to, someone to hear their story, to walk with them through their fears and pain. At their weakest point, they just want someone to affirm that they have not always been this way, that their lives and self-worth are so much more than their experience in the hospital.

As ministers, this is what we are training to do. While everyone we meet will obviously not be on their deathbed facing a dramatic existential crisis, many will be faced with issues they've never had to deal with before. Insecurity. Fear. Doubt. Weakness. Boredom. Regret. Pain. Disillusionment. As ministers, it is our role to be with them, to hear them, and to restore hope in them.

And this is by no means easy. In fact, I imagine it will be the most difficult thing I do in my life. But I think I learned a valuable lesson on my first day: The first step in helping someone restore hope is to discover and lift up who the patient knows him/herself to be at their best, not who they are at their weakest, sitting before us. If all we can see is the sickness or infirmity affecting the person, we will never be able to see the whole person before us, and thus, we will never be able to help them in the way they need. That's quite a lesson to learn on the first day, and quite a task for the year. But if God can use an unconscious man to speak to me so well on just the first day, I know that God is capable of working through even me.

I first started to get excited about my faith in high school when my family moved to a parish that had an active youth group. Inspired by the amazing energy of the group and the intensity of work and worship they shared each week, I found myself "on fire" for the Church. Beyond what was required for confirmation, I attended youth group meetings *because I wanted to be there*, became a peer minister, helped plan retreats, volunteered on service projects, and often led people in praise and worship, skits, activities, and small group discussions. I loved every minute of it, and even though I had to graduate from high school, I did not want it to end. And why did it have to? I was on my way to college where there would surely be a Catholic organization to join. Before arriving on campus my freshman year, I emailed the president of Catholic Campus Ministry and told her how excited I was to get started, all the things I could do, and ideas I had for the program.

That's right. I offered ideas to the leader before even meeting her.

Almost immediately upon setting foot on campus I found that their program was nothing like what I had experienced in high school. Disappointed but not discouraged, I tried to step right in and offer suggestions, even leading a trial event modeled exactly like the events I knew from high school. This did not go well. No one showed up but the president, a few team members, and a friend of mine that helped plan it. A bit discouraged at that point, I had a conversation with the campus minister that I will never forget. He affirmed my enthusiasm and told me not to let it go; one day I would be a really important leader in the group. But not right now. He asked if I could step back a bit, take in what was already going on all around me, and start by being an active participant who listened and watched before leading. Maybe, he suggested, there was something different about college ministry than my high school youth group, and I needed to let myself grow into that understanding before taking charge.

Such an obvious insight, and yet so often needed: You need to listen before you speak.

One of the biggest problems I have found in religious life—in my life and in others—is a desire to step in and fix things immediately. Call it a savior complex, call it clericalism, call it the result of simply being asked to help people all day every day, there is definitely a tendency in professional ministry to jump right in with a solution. Educated in theology, trained in counseling, and spending our whole lives in and around the Church, we just want to care for people, and for the most part, are pretty good at it. When people come to us in pain and are looking for guidance, we want to give it.

And there is nothing wrong with that in itself. But it is not the first step: We have to listen.

As a professor of mine used to say, "Get below what they are saying and listen for what they are *actually* saying." Someone may appear a certain way, express a long list of issues, ask for help with something particular, or even claim that they are fine. But what is below their outward appearance? What do they *actually* need? Truly, who are they before God? Before entering novitiate—a year in which candidates of varying levels of commitment and maturity come together for intense preparation, often causing many fraternal problems—a long-time friar gave me some excellent advice: No matter what people do or what you may think of them, try with all your heart to see them as Jesus sees them. He said—and he was right—that there would be men who are difficult to live with and that I would wonder why they were even in this life. Look beyond the exterior and try to understand what Jesus knows and why they might have been called to live this life.

When (if) we are able to do that, what we find might surprise us.

Sometimes, when we are humble enough to listen without immediately judging or stepping in to fix the situation, we might find that what we first found to be broken, incomplete, dirty, or unwanted is in fact a beautiful witness to God's glory. How many times in Scripture did God choose the lowly and overlooked to be his messenger? Sarah was too old. Moses did not speak well. Jeremiah was too young. Mary Magdalene had seven demons. Nothing good could come from Galilee, they said. And look what God did to the rich and the proud through them. Who or what in our world might we overlook when we have all the answers, when we speak first before we listen? Whether it is freshman-in-college me who wants to lead before I even know what I am leading, or a skilled and seasoned minister counseling someone through an issue they have dealt with hundreds of times before, we never have the whole picture; we can never know who or what God is going to use to teach us something new. If we truly want to build up the kingdom of God, we must have the eyes and ears of that kingdom, and the humility to accept that we do not always have the answer. If what we do allows us to do that, we might be well on our way to a vocation.

But we are not done.

Once we have listened to the world as God would have us listen and have determined what it needs from us, there is still a question of how we do it. In my experience, and what I suggest as our second principle, is that we must lead *with*, not *above* or *apart* from those we serve.

This post, written while in temporary profession and engaged in active ministry, recalls how being a strong leader means more than simply being successful, and that, as ministers in the Church, our goal must be as much people-oriented as it is task-oriented.

I Can Do It!

When I was a senior in college, I had the great privilege of acting as our club baseball team's president. Since there was no active faculty involved with the team, that meant that I was also the coach. Between the vice president and myself, we petitioned for money from the school, recruited people to sign up, ran practices, paid for regular expenses, and coached games. It was an incredible experience with incredible results. We went 13-2 in the regular season (good enough to win our division), then went 3-1 in the regional tournament, earning a berth to the Club Baseball World Series in Pennsylvania—this from a team that had gone 0-7 and 6-4 in the previous two years! Even though we didn't play well in the World Series, it was a storybook end to my baseball career and one of the fondest memories I will ever have.

At the time, I was very proud of myself. Naturally, I was proud of the whole team, but I really did work hard to make us successful. While the vice president definitely helped, I felt that it was my ambition, persistence, and creativity that fueled the team. The budget I submitted was detailed and professional (which led to us receiving the third highest budget of any team, a huge increase from the year before), I got people to actually come to practice twice a week (more than six once a week was a success in previous years), found an abandoned baseball field near the school and worked to clean it up for practices (the previous two years we practiced on a community soccer field), convinced the varsity baseball coach to let us use the school's batting cages on their off day (restoring a relationship that had been ruined years before by a previous club president), and didn't stop recruiting until the final week of roster closures (the week we picked up our starting RF/#2 hitter, and a defunct varsity pitcher). At the time, as I said, I was proud of myself.

That was until I checked in with the team the year after I left. When I left, they were set up to repeat and had real reason to think that they would be even more successful. In essence, they lost me, another senior who only played in the final weekend, and our number 3 pitcher. They still had their top two pitchers (one was probably the best pitcher in the division, and the other guy finished with an ERA under 1.00 the year before), still had their entire lineup save the #3 hitter, and had an entire class of new freshmen coming in. So what happened? Did they repeat and go to the World Series? No. They finished below .500, had to forfeit a number of games, and missed the playoffs entirely.

When I lamented about this to a friend, he thought I was bragging, as if to say, "Look how much they needed me. They couldn't do anything without me." That wasn't my first thought. When I saw the immediate drop in results with almost no loss in talent, I realized that I had actually failed them in setting up the team for the long run.

I think a problem we all have when we are passionate about something and want to make it successful is an "I can do it" attitude. What do I mean by this? I'm not talking about initiative or confidence in oneself; this sort of "I can do it" attitude is something all leaders need. Rather, I'm talking about the sort of "I can do it" attitude that does not include others in the building process, in a sense saying, "If I don't do it, it won't get done right." Sometimes it is an issue of control and lack of trust in others; other times it is simply a failure to identify talents in others and offer them opportunities to succeed even if "I can do it" better. I think my attitude was somewhere in between the two.

For me, this was my last shot at playing baseball and I made it my highest priority. Was I really going to take chances with guys who weren't as passionate?

And it was successful...for one year. What I did was make sure everything was done right; what I failed to do was empower anyone else to care to do it that way once I was gone.

As friars, it can be very tempting to lead our ministries in this way. And who can blame us? In many cases, we're often the most capable of doing any job around the parish: We're passionate about our ministry and want it to do well, are highly trained with graduate degrees and many years of preparation, and are definitely the most responsible if something were to go wrong. "If I can do it, why wouldn't I? It is my job." Add a generally likable personality to the mix, and there's almost a guarantee for success.

But what happens when a) that specific friar is transferred to a new fraternity, b) a parishioner moves to another church not run by an "I can do it" priest, or, God forbid, c) we have to turn the ministry back over to the diocese because we can no longer staff it? If all we have ever done is lead from the top, making all of the decisions and making sure everything is done "perfectly," if all we have ever done has been to lead with an "I can do it" (so no one else has to) attitude, then the people we serve will never know that they can do it too.

And they can.

I admire our friars who do this so well, leading with the people they serve as the people they serve, empowering them to take an active part in leadership. Because, when you think about it, we are shepherds, not CEOs. We are not owners or kings; we are guides and supporters. The Church does not belong to us nor does it require us to function properly. It belongs to the people of God, and it is our role to make sure they are passionate about and capable of taking up their own cross, not to make sure it is successful at all costs.

Coaching baseball for one year in college will no doubt be one of my fondest memories for the rest of my life because of our success, but it will also be one of the most important memories for me in effective leadership. If all we want are short-term gains, do it ourselves; if we want to make something lasting and worthwhile, we have to build people up and empower them to lead it with us. Coaching that year taught me that "I can do it" can certainly lead to success, but the sort of success I really desire can only be won with an attitude of "we can do it!"

It turns out that the campus minister was right my freshman year, and I did end up becoming an important part of Catholic Campus Ministry. The next year I was elected as retreat coordinator and the following two years as program director, both newly created positions. Unfortunately, this was before my experience coaching the club baseball team, and I had not yet learned how important it was to include others in the process. Meeting one evening my junior year with the leadership team, I presented the plan for our upcoming retreat. Passionate, vigilant, and concerned with every detail, I had everything laid out. Theme. Timeline. Activities. Talks. Transitions. Free time. Everything had a purpose and everything was thoughtfully planned as a part of the overall work of the retreat. It was a good plan that simply needed to be approved.

Or so I thought.

Almost universally, the team rejected some part of the plan. There were complaints about this or that, requests to move something to another place, and new ideas for activities. With too much disagreement to get the plan passed quickly, I took out a marker and started marking up the schedule. I listened to everything that was said and rearranged the schedule to accommodate their concerns. After an hour or so of discussions and replanning, we had come full circle and *ended up all agreeing on the original plan we started with.*

Yup. That is an hour and a half I will never get back.

But here is the thing: I had no room to complain. I had failed to allow anyone else to own what we were all going to do and deserved the pushback I received. I had made the plan *my* plan. The theme was *my* theme. Essentially, the retreat was *my* retreat. Implicitly or explicitly, my presentation to the group said that I did not want their opinion, that their contributions were not necessary. When we worked out the details *together* and the team was able to see why everything was put together as it was and to contribute in the process, the plan made much more sense. It was now *our* retreat that we could experience together, not just *my* retreat that they could attend.

This process may not be as efficient as working on our own, but that is what being Church is.

St. Paul writes in the letter to the Galatians that in Christ, "There is neither Jew nor Greek, there is neither slave nor free person, there is not male and female; for you are all one in Christ Jesus." While on earth and in the institutional Church there are obviously those who have been set aside for particular duties and so have a role in the *ministerial* priesthood (deacons, priests, and bishops through ordination), the

Second Vatican Council reminds us that our primary identity as Christians is in our *baptismal* priesthood and that it is this identity, not our ministerial one, that defines and unites our work together in the Church. A priest is not better or more important than the congregation but is called *from* the community of baptized to serve *with* his fellow brothers and sisters in Christ. Before and more essential than any role or ordination one may have in the Church is the one baptism of faith that unites and strengthens us all.

It is because of this that *all* of us—not just those ordained to the ministerial priesthood, those who are educated in theology, people we like, work the way we do, and agree with us—are responsible for building up the Church and the efforts of the kingdom of God. As ministers, it is not up to us who gets to contribute; as lay people, it is not up to us whether we want to get involved. Through our baptism, *all* of us have a role to play. Internally, the Mass is not the exclusive purview of the priest, something that the faithful are subject to and watch from afar. No, the Second Vatican Council reminds us that from our baptism we are *all* called to "full and active participation" in the liturgy (*Sacrosanctum Concilium*, 14), that the liturgy truly is the work *of* and *for* the people. Externally, the work of the Church in the world is not the responsibility of only those who have consecrated their lives to the Church. No, the Second Vatican Council reminds us that from our baptism we are *all* called to witness to Christ's threefold ministry in the world, praying for and offering our lives as a spiritual sacrifice like a *priest*, announcing the kingdom and teaching the world about God like a *prophet*, and leading with justice and promoting peace in our world like a *king*.

As much as we may want to exclude some for the sake of efficiency or personal glory, or as much as we may want to pass on the responsibility because of self-doubt or apathy, we do not have that right. The kingdom of God needs to be built by all of us working together as one. The *world* needs this example from us.

But again, this is not all the world needs. Once we have listened enough to know what we need to do, and once we have begun to do it in a way that promotes active community involvement, there is one more essential principle needed: We need to live with an evangelical spirit that joyfully shares what we have found with others. This post, written during my third year of studies, addresses one of the most obvious symbols of this in our Church.

Do the Clothes Make the Man?

You've heard this phrase before, I'm sure. For many, it expresses the very strong link people make between the way someone looks and his or her worth in society. Well-dressed people are important and poorly dressed people are not. For the most part, it is a fairly superficial statement.

But what if the clothes actually did make people who they were? In discussing the symbolic importance of clothing in my Pentateuch class this week, our professor shared a rather fascinating study published in 2012 called "Enclothed Cognition." Basically, researches gave two groups of graduate students the exact same white coats to wear and asked them to complete a series of cognitive tasks. One group was told that the white coat was a doctor's lab coat, the other was told that it was a painter's coat. The results? Those who believed they were wearing a lab coat made half as many mistakes as those who believed they were wearing a painter's coat!

As the article says, researchers have known for years that the way one looks can affect the way people are perceived and treated. What this study indicates, though, is that the clothing one wears can actually affect one's image of self, and thus, have an effect on one's psychological processes and productivity.

I have long been a believer of this, even before knowing the science behind it. In high school, our baseball coach allowed us to wear anything we wanted to practice as long as we had long pants and our shirts represented the school. Almost every player chose to wear sweatpants and an untucked t-shirt. I just couldn't. I wore baseball pants, high socks, belt, and tucked in baseball shirt, the same things I wore for actual games. To most of them, it didn't matter what one wore, it was how one played that mattered. Which is true. But at least for me, I knew that how I dressed affected how I played. Besides the obvious practical concerns (sweatpants are more cumbersome than baseball pants) there was a psychological disposition that clothing had on me: In my mind, wearing sweatpants was associated with lounging around and being lazy, whereas wearing baseball pants was associated with playing baseball, something that was always done as hard as I could, and helped me focus. Clothing was not an inconsequential external, it was a conscious decision that changed the way I thought about myself and likely affected my psychological disposition.

As someone in religious life, this sort of insight is very interesting to me. While I get the feeling that the issue of wearing a religious habit is completely irrelevant to most people, it is a question that has been hotly contested by priests and religious since the Second Vatican Council. Should we wear distinct religious garb? Because there are such strong opinions on either side, the general conclusion for many is simply to say, "It doesn't matter what you wear anyway, so wear whatever you want."

I disagreed with this notion when I played baseball, and now, having learned that there is actual research in this area, have to disagree again. What one wears is not some inconsequential external with no meaning. It is an expression of oneself with significant import. What one wears not only affects how one is treated, it affects the way that we understand ourselves and act in the world. As public figures concerned with the spiritual and physical well-being of all people, called to evangelize and shepherd God's people, how could this not matter?

But that doesn't mean I'm calling for everyone to wear their habits and collars. Actually, in what might be the biggest surprise for some people, it's quite the opposite: I think some people should wear their habits much less.

Yeah. Didn't see that coming, did you?

Here's what I mean. For me, the habit is a positive sign. It symbolizes humility, connects me to the larger tradition and Church, allows me to connect with the people of God, and overall, makes me feel good as a pastoral minister. I embody what my clothes mean to me. But what about those friars for which the habit represents something negative, a sign of privilege or a way to separate the laity from ministers? For them, wearing the habit and embodying what it means to them is not going to allow them to be the best ministers they can be. Or, worse yet, what about those people for whom the habit is a sign of privilege and a way to separate the laity from ministers, and they like that about it? What it causes them to embody is extremely detrimental to the faith.

So, I guess the question I have comes down to this: If

clothes can actually "make the man," what sort of man is his religious garb making him into? If what someone wears makes him or her a less effective minister or moves them further from God, it might be time for a wardrobe change.

In most novitiates, friars are invested in a habit upon being received on the first day; although not yet in vows, novices are considered temporary members of the order and so are normally given the habit like the rest of the brothers. This was not the case in my novitiate. For whatever reason, the novitiate team decided to develop a series of stages throughout the year so to gradually enter us into the process, and so "divestiture" (previously mentioned), receiving the rule of St. Francis, and "investiture" were separated into special rituals throughout the year. This meant that I was technically a friar for four months without any visible sign of such. I wore the clothes I wore in college.

A few years later I was reflecting on this experience with an older friar and shared that there was something about it that did not sit right with me. I told him, "Even though I was living the life of a friar, I did not *feel* like I was really a friar until I received my habit." To a man of his generation, this was not the right thing to say. "There is more to being a friar than wearing the habit," he snapped at me, disgusted that I would say such a thing. For him, the habit was nothing more than an outdated costume that represented a different world and distracted from the true meaning of being a friar.

And I get that. Truly I do. But I just see it a little differently.

I think it goes without saying that wearing the habit is an important part of my vocation. Besides the fact that "Breaking in the Habit" is the name of my blog and YouTube channel, wearing the habit was a major consideration in my discernment process and has become central to my vocation as a Franciscan. But it has nothing to do with capturing the nostalgia of an earlier time, wanting an elevated status or special treatment, or simply because I want the attention, as some perceive in others; that sort of clericalism is out there and certainly on the rise among young vocations, but it does not describe me one bit. For me, the habit is a sign of radical availability and evangelization. When I put it on and go out into the world, yes, I do attract more attention to myself than I otherwise would, but ultimately the attention does not go to *me*, it goes to what I represent; it is not my face or my person that people remember when they encounter me, it is the Church, a "holy man," a brother, someone who can help them. When I put the habit on and go out into the world, I am no longer me, Casey Cole, with my set of personal needs and desires, I am a herald of the kingdom and a servant of the world, ready and willing to accept anything that comes my way.

Oh, and it does come my way.

When I am in the habit out in the world—shopping at the grocery store, going to class, riding the bus, whatever—I am approached by the widest variety of people. Some come asking for prayers, comfortably revealing to a complete stranger their deepest desires and most difficult struggles. Others want to tell me about how they used to be Catholic but left for whatever reason. A few have taken the opportunity to tell me how they feel about religion and how I am bad for the world. Most are simply curious about what I am wearing and why. In

WHAT THE WORLD NEEDS

each situation, even in those that seem confrontational and displeasing, I have an opportunity to work for the kingdom of God. Shopping at a grocery store, going to class, riding a bus—in all of these places, without doing anything but remaining open and present, I am able to engage people where they are and offer them a bit of my faith.

As a novice in jeans, I could not do that and that was a real detriment to my vocation.

Does this mean that every religious should wear a habit? Are visible signs of medieval concepts really what the world needs today? Absolutely not. But it does need *some* visible presence of the radical counter-cultural message of the Gospel. When the Church told religious orders that they no longer needed to wear distinguished garb, recognizing that the modern world required flexibility to carry out the mission, it did not intend for communities to begin acting as secret agents. I met a sister once who was very proud that she had worked in a hospital for more than twenty years before someone knew she was a sister. Knowing what she meant—that she was proud of the fact that she did not need a title or distinct garb to live the Gospel and that her love for the people she served was what really mattered—I could not help but feel more than a bit disheartened by her statement. *Twenty years had gone by without anyone knowing why you served and where your strength came from.* Something is missing in that vocation.

Of all that I have ever read from the official Church, it is difficult to think of something that has been more inspiring in my life than Pope Francis's apostolic exhortation, *Evangelii Guadium*. Isn't that what our life is ultimately about, the "joy of the Gospel"? Our life and mission as Christians, he reminds us, is to daily have a personal encounter with Jesus Christ in such a way that we can do nothing more than go out into the world with joy and confidence in our message. We are not called to be safe and hide within our houses; we are not to go only to those who will accept our message without trial; we are not to go out half-convinced of what we share, appearing as "sourpusses." No! The joy of the Gospel is something that cannot be contained or suppressed, does not fear being bruised or dirty, and knows that *everyone* deserves to hear that message.

Habit or not, visible symbol or casual attire, *this* is the attitude that the world needs from us and what every vocation requires at its core. No matter how we do it or what we look like when we do, the most important thing that we can ever do is to live with so much love for the triune God that it is reflected in our lives for others to receive. The truth and hope of Christianity have become so familiar to some, so distant to others, that it no longer gives meaning to people in difficult situations. All around the world people are looking for meaning and finding it in strange, even destructive places. The world does not need secret servants and incognito ministers, holding onto what they have found and hiding it under a bushel basket. The world needs men and women who are so in love and so convinced of the truth that they cannot help but share it with others in word and deed, that they cannot help but make Christ present in the world. More than anything else, if what we do enables us to live with evangelical zeal for the sake of the world—even if what we do is long-distance pogo stick juggling—we just might be doing what we are called to do.

Listen with the ears; see with the eyes of God.

Work together to build up the kingdom.

And share what we have found with the world.

These are the things that the world needs, and so these are the things that we as Christians need to devote ourselves to doing. Of course, following this path will not lead us to all to any one thing, but together with the two questions from the opening chapter, we have enough of a guide, I think, to find our calling. For me, as well as for hundreds of thousands of others for the past eight hundred years, these three things come together in one convenient answer: a renewed Franciscan spirituality in our world. This final post, written in 2016, looks at four things that made the Franciscan movement spread like wildfire in the thirteenth century and asks if our world might be ripe for another revolution.

What the World Needs

1. A renewed sense of prayer. When we think of the medieval world, many of us think that everyone was Christian, that it was not until the modern world that "secular society" began to exist. The fact of the matter is that there has always been a divide between the religious and secular, and Christians have had various degrees of religious commitment since the time of Jesus. In Francis's time, corruption (both at the hands of the Church and civil society), disenfranchisement, and apathy were all around. Few people received the Eucharist, and because many people were either illiterate or ignored, they rarely had profound encounters with God in the Church.

With Francis and the Franciscans, the Church was called to a renewed sense of prayer and spirituality. Their "incarnational spirituality" showed people that God was in their midst, comprehendible and accessible to them wherever they were. And do you know what? They used entertainment to get their message across. The Franciscans were popular preachers. They did not preach precise doctrines or theological treatises; they preached the Gospel in the language of their hearers. They preached with joy, with life, and most of all, with creativity. Their spirituality caused people to change their lives, but their style of preaching made people want to listen to them in the first place.

Today, the world looks quite different, but the issues remain the same: Many people are disconnected, alienated, even cynical towards faith. But notice how I don't say that it is "secular society" or "new atheism" that's the problem. While more and more people are claiming "no preference" on religion, there is still a strong spiritual yearning, even among youth. The real problem, as I see it, is that the established religions have failed to speak the language of new generations and engage them in a way that makes prayer meaningful. Too often, when faced with difficult questions, they're handed answers of morality and philosophy when all they're looking for is compassion, inspiration, and joy.

How do we respond? With engaging preaching that comes from a solid life in prayer. For Francis, the world was his cloister: He could at once be grounded in prayer while also attuned to the needs of the people around him, a witness to something greater.

2. Brought together in equality. The thirteenth century saw the beginnings of a new economic system: The feudal economy was fading away, and the market economy was coming into prominence. On the one hand, it brought wealth to people who would have otherwise been ignored because of their lack of nobility; on the other hand, it broke the bonds of responsibility for the poor and subjected some to even more humiliating poverty. It was a time of major class division, growing disparity between rich and poor, and no recourse to bridge the gap.

And then there were the Franciscans. Here was this bunch of men that brought together rich and poor at one table: clergy, professors, princes, homeless, porters, lepers. Together in one family, they were all equal. Where else in the thirteenth century could you experience such radical emphasis on human dignity? Where could you step outside of the expectations and systems of society to live as the apostles did? Nowhere.

Today, we see the divide between the rich and poor growing rapidly in recent years. In the past forty years, the United States has seen some of the worst of this: The top 1 percent own 10 percent more of the total wealth today than they did in 1979, have seen a 275 percent increase in income compared to 40 percent for the rest, and in 2011, despite being the most affluent country in the world, half of the people in the United States lived in poverty or were designated low-income. Among the rest of the world, the United States is in the 30th percentile (70 percent of countries are better) with the trend getting worse.

How do we respond? By being minors for the sake of the poor. Because we do not believe that we are above anyone else or deserve respect because of who we are, we find ourselves among the poorest and most forgotten of society.

3. A fraternity bigger than oneself. I can't say exactly what it was about the time of Francis, but there appeared to be a deep yearning for brotherhood. Francis and his brothers were by no means revolutionary when it came to the idea of forming a brotherhood. The Middle Ages saw a tremendous flux of new communities and orders all throughout the Church. The answer might be a simple one: People have a natural drive to be together, and seeing other people with similar ambitions is attractive.

Today, we live in a highly individualized culture. In a very positive way, the turn to the self has allowed more people to develop a personal relationship with Jesus in a way that previous generations simply did not even think about, not to mention the heightened sense of the personal dignity and health of self. These are great things. That said, much of our culture has taken this to the extreme, isolating and individualizing everything in such a way that we live fragmented, selfish lives. Everything is about "me, me, me." The rise of new forms of communication have connected people in ways never before seen, but it has not been accompanied with the maturity and responsibility required to maintain personal relationship at the same time. Despite being so connected, so much of the world feels so alone.

How do we respond? With an example of "us, us, us." Being a fraternity in mission categorically changes the way we do mission, and really, the mission itself. We don't just work together, together we work for the sake of one another; we don't just live together, we have lives together.

4. Building bridges, not walls. Finally, there could be no discussion about the Franciscans without a mention of peacefulness. One of the most foundational experiences in Francis's own conversion was witnessing the horrors of war. In his time, there were battles between cities, wars between nations, and a little thing called the crusades. Groups like the "Knights Templar" and "Militia of the Faith of Jesus Christ" (seriously...) even sprang up as religious brotherhoods of soldiers, seeing it their duty to engage in violence for the sake of the kingdom.

The Franciscans could not be any more different. Francis always came in peace and told his brothers to always begin preaching with the words, "Peace be with you." They were forbidden to carry arms and could not even use violence to defend their own property or lives. As if this were not revolutionary enough, Francis even went to the front lines of the Crusades and attempted to make peace. Crossing enemy lines, he walked right into the camp of the Muslims and spoke with the sultan. Did he tell the sultan that Islam was wrong? No. Did he try to convert the sultan? Nope. He simply showed the love he had for God and spoke with him as a brother. Even in his words, Francis acted as a man of peace before all.

Today, violence is all around us. It is on battlefields, in our streets, on our televisions, in our politics, and in our homes. It's as if we have forgotten how to dialogue, how to disagree with one another while maintaining respect. In the political debates leading up to the 2016 election, we have seen a prime example of this. But it's more than that. Washington is not broken as much as Washington reflects the way we engage one another in our daily lives: name-calling, judging, excluding "those" people, looking down on those with whom we disagree, and failing to show each other the respect we deserve.

How do we respond? By being peacemakers like St. Francis. Rather than seeing everyone as potential enemies, why not see everyone as Francis did, fellow children of God? Instead of starting conflicts or running from them, why not run toward them with a desire to reconcile? We need peacemakers who are willing to build bridges, not walls.

Eight hundred years ago, the Franciscan Order grew like wildfire because it was exactly what the world needed and people wanted to be a part of the movement. Today, I think that is still the case. What we stand for is exactly what the world is longing for.

But ideals and mission statements don't change the world. Throughout history, it has been the men and women who have heard the call and lived these values that has made the real difference. Nothing else will do.

So, what does the world need today? It needs men and women who live prayerful lives, lives that spring forth in creative in relatable ways; it needs men and women who are able to check their ambition and privilege at the door to be equals with anyone else who walks in; it needs men and women who are capable of struggling with others, overcoming their shortcomings, and making it work with others; it needs men and women who want to live for others, who want to build the kingdom of God even in the most difficult of places.

The funny thing about it all is that these people are already out there in the world, living and doing these very things. Maybe it's even you. Maybe what the world needs most right now is not some politician to fix our problems or God to perform some incredible miracle, but you, as you are, living the eight-hundred-year-old charism of St. Francis of Assisi.

Yes. Maybe that is exactly what the world needs: more Franciscans. More people to live with the radical love of St. Francis, to leave everything behind and "rebuild" the Church with humility and joy. In consecrated vowed life, cloistered contemplative life, and even in married secular life, the Franciscan charism has found a home in hundreds of thousands of people over the years. Maybe now is time for another rebirth of that charism.

If it is—if we are to be followers and imitators of St. Francis—then the thing we need above all is the humility to know that people do not need us: They need Jesus. Francis never wanted anyone to follow him, he wanted them to follow *the one he followed.* "The Lord has shown me what is mine to do. May he show you what is yours." In this humility, we realize that it is not our strength, our ingenuity, our love, or our care that is going to shape the world. It is Jesus that the world needs, working through us.

The world does not need *us*. It needs someone who will bring it Jesus.

Thank God. Because, really, we could never do anything well on our own. As hard as we try and no matter the intentions we have, the truth of the matter is that sometimes we fail. Actually, we fail a lot. We fail the world, we fail our brothers and sisters, and we fail ourselves. If we truly want to be what the world needs, we need to accept that we are not its savior and that it is actually in our weakness and failing that Christ is made strong in us and in the world.

· · · · · ·

chapter six

Sometimes We Fail

Here would be a nice place to end. Having taken the time to step away *from* the world in discernment and prayer to lay a foundation in God, and stretched beyond one's comfort zone in relationship with others and in minority to broaden one's perspective *of* the world, we are finally and triumphantly sent out *into* the world on a mission. Led to fulfill a Godly task and equipped with all we need for the journey, we reach the end of our trial and are ready to sail off into the sunset. We have found something that brings us joy, we are good at, and the world needs. We are ready to live happily ever after living out our call. The end.

Right...

As much as this *would* be a nice place to end, and as strange as it may seem to end a book on such a seemingly down note like failure, my Christian and Franciscan life has shown me that there is often more to the story than happily ever after. Sometimes, despite our best intentions and highest hopes, we find what we believe to be our calling only to have it fail miserably before us. Even in the work of the kingdom, things do not always go as we plan. In my junior year of college, I ran for president of Catholic Campus Ministry; despite being a passionate member of the group, a religion major, and called to a lifetime of ministry to the Church, I was not elected. Two years ago I spent a summer in Mexico at a refugee camp; despite the effort I put in, the desire I had to serve those in need, and my willingness to step *way* outside of my comfort zone, I did not learn much Spanish, was almost entirely unable to help people, and contracted an infection that was the most painful experience of my life. Last year, I headed a group from the parish to resettle a refugee family in our area; despite a large corps of volunteers, a sophisticated communication system, and countless hours of organization and volunteering, our contract with the sponsoring organization was terminated over a personality dispute. Time and time again, all I wanted to do was to serve God and yet faced adversity and trial preventing me from doing so.

Why, we might ask, do bad things happen to good people? When we finally decide to give up ourselves and everything we have to serve God, why do we continue to experience so much suffering?

No doubt an age-old philosophical question—of which I have no intention of sufficiently answering here. My basic response is to ask a question of my own: As Christians, followers of the innocent God-man who ended his life in suffering and humiliation for the sake of others, why would we expect *less* suffering in this life than in any other? Seriously. The central act of our savior was his *death*. The symbol of our religion is *an instrument of execution*. While Jesus did tell his disciples, "My yoke is easy, and my burden light," and although his final words to them commissioned them to go out and joyfully announce the kingdom, we cannot forget the foundation for their evangelism: the cross. Jesus is the Good Shepherd that laid down his life for the sheep and called his disciples to do the same. He tells them, "My cup you will indeed drink," and "You will be hated by all because of my name." Jesus sent the disciples out to do extraordinary and fulfilling work, and he calls us today to continue in that ministry, but at the core of who we are we preach Christ crucified.

Sometimes we forget that taking up our own crosses daily is central to living as a follower of Jesus. Wanting to focus only on the nice and extraordinary aspects of our faith—jumping right to Easter Sunday—we forget that the joy of Easter is not possible without the trial and pain of Good Friday. Sometimes, being a "good Christian" and wanting to serve God does not free us from this unfortunate reality...it leads us directly into it.

Never have I known this more than on Good Friday itself, three years ago. Asked to give a reflection at an evening service, all I wanted to do was to share my faith and help people understand the mystery of the cross. All I got was the most humiliating experience of my life. This post, written two days after the event, is a reflection on that horrible evening.

Sometimes We Fail

Last year, I wrote *The Joy of Our Salvation* as a candid recounting of the Easter Vigil, calling it "hands-down the best liturgical experience I have ever had." I was amazed by the transcendence of the liturgy, the energy in the congregation, the faith in the catechumens. Last year, everything went exactly as planned. It was an incredible success.

This year went a little differently.

Now a theology student with a little experience preaching, I was asked by the pastor of St. Camillus Church to give the English "reflection" for Good Friday, the celebration of the Lord's passion. I was honored. I was excited. Those who know me know that I love big liturgies and I love to preach. Come Friday morning, I felt really great about what I wrote and couldn't wait to share it with a packed church on such an important day.

But things did not go according to plan. Starting around four o'clock that afternoon, I developed a headache which turned out to be a migraine. I was in pain and confused for a few hours. I felt dizzy and disoriented for much of the afternoon. I could see, but part of my vision was blurry. I took a long nap, got some medicine and right before the service started I felt a little better. Rather than have the pastor stand up and have to make something up, I decided to give it my best. I would be in a little pain but thought that I could still do a decent job.

I didn't.

In front of my fellow student friars, four priests, and an almost packed church that included friends, strangers, and even one of my professors, I failed miserably. Within twenty seconds I lost my place. After a few sentences, I became downright confused. Looking directly at my written reflection, I could see the words but they meant absolutely nothing to me. I said one sentence a few times because it seemed completely incoherent. Three times I stopped, caught my breath and tried again. I looked at my paper again, but they were only nonsense words. I couldn't do it. After three tries and about two minutes of embarrassment, I looked at the pastor, said "I'm sorry," and began to cry as I walked away. I made it to the sacristy, fell to the floor, and cried as hard as I ever had.

I had failed.

I hope that this doesn't come off too dramatic or even privileged, but it was easily one of the worst experiences of my life. Not only was I in a good bit of pain, I embarrassed the heck out of myself, messed up the liturgy, and back in the sacristy, my classmates, two priests, and some strangers saw me crying, something I have not let people see in many years. How could this have gone any worse?

But then a friar sent me a text and my perspective began to change ever so slightly:

"In no way should you feel embarrassed. It was incredibly brave for you to try to do it. I'm very proud of you for trying to tough it out, but also knowing when to ask for help. While I'm sorry you had to go through it, I think for most folks it was a rather poignant demonstration of what carrying the cross looks like in real life. Several people said to tell you what a beautiful homily it was. And it truly was."

By most definitions, what I did up there was anything but a success. I stumbled. I lost my place. I didn't even get one third of the way finished before I quit. And yet, the result was anything but a failure. There before me, I witnessed my brother stepping in to finish my words for me. I felt my classmates and random members of the choir come to bring me water and console me (like, ten people crowded in the sacristy within seconds!) Some even mentioned later that the abruptness of the situation broke them out of the predictable pattern and awoke them to something more before them. How could it be that I was unable to do anything right, that the plan failed miserably, and yet Christ's message came through?

God transforms our failures into his success.

I stood up, relying on my own strength, thinking that I was going to talk about the pain Jesus went through, the humiliation he experienced, and how he even wept, but my strength was not enough. I couldn't do it by myself. And I didn't have to. There we were celebrating the moment in history when Christ triumphantly took our pain and weakness upon himself, subsumed our failures into his perfection, and it began unfolding once again before our eyes. I wanted to talk about this event, but God wanted to show it. My weakness was turned into strength, my failure into success. The Paschal mystery could not be contained by words.

To say that this year's Triduum celebration went off without a hitch would be far from the truth. Before my Easter this year, I had to experience one of the most difficult crosses of my life. Nobody likes to realize that they are not strong enough. Nobody likes to admit that sometimes we fail.

But we do. And that's okay.

It is in our weakness that Christ is our strength. It is in our failings that Christ is our success. It is in the crosses we bear that Christ is our Easter joy. May we never be ashamed of our weaknesses, despairing over our failures, or refuse to carry our crosses. Sometimes we fail. Every time Christ succeeds. Happy Easter! Alleluia!

One thing that most people will not tell you about religious life is that we take *a lot* of personality inventories and psychological tests. And for good reason. If we are going to enter into the lives of others and hope to be of any help, we need to understand what we bring to the situation, both positively and negatively. What about my personal makeup might bias my ability to serve effectively? We all have our weak spots and our troubled areas, and knowing what they are can only be helpful.

In my case, I have a tremendous aversion to failure. A classic "3" on the Enneagram (the "Achiever"), I am driven by a desire to be successful, both individually and collectively, and I put a lot of weight in tangible accomplishments. I am a task-oriented community organizer that is able to get the most out of people for the sake of the mission, coordinate many details at once, and be a presentable, confident leader in the face of challenges. At my best, I am motivated to work cooperatively with others, seeing my relationships as the most important task at hand, and am comfortable being vulnerable with others.

If only we could always be at our best.

At my worst, my desire to be successful becomes internalized and I begin to think that my worth is tied to my productivity, "People will like me if I am good at something," or much worse, the opposite: "People will *not* like me if I am a failure." Thus, at my worst, failure is not an option, and I will do anything—lie to myself or others, quit, avoid the situation, or make excuses—to avoid accepting that I might be the reason something went wrong.

You can imagine, then, how my experience of Good Friday might have been intensified with such baggage. In my mind, all I could see was that I did not complete the task. I disrupted the liturgy. Not only did I look less-than-presentable, *people saw me when I was weak and broken.* My humiliation was not just the sort of thing that everyone else goes through, it defeated me at my very core. *How could someone love me when I am so worthless?*

And yet they still did. More, in fact.

I cannot tell you how many people came up to me in the days after wanting to make sure I was all right. They did not care about the homily, they had forgotten all about the liturgy, and all they were concerned with was my well-being. *But, I'm a failure...aren't you embarrassed to be with me? Don't you think less of me?* In the case of one brother, it was quite the opposite. In a bit of candid honesty, he shared weeks later that it was actually in that moment that he first began to think of me as a friend. Prior to seeing me so vulnerable and weak, he told me, all he had ever seen of me was someone who always seemed so put together and confident, and for him, *that* was actually off-putting. *How strange,* I thought. *People care about me for who I am, not what I do, and may even like me more in my failure.* It was as if, as crazy as it sounds, failure could bring about success.

You know, like the essence of Christianity that I was trying to preach about.

It was in failure—not in joyful success—that I came to understand the power of God's grace, that even when we fail God still succeeds. In the Paschal Mystery, the dying and rising of Jesus Christ, we see that God does not just *permit* weakness and failure, God *transforms* those things into successes for the kingdom. But it is more than just this one extraordinary act. In everything we do and in everything we are, God continues to work through us—even when we fail—to bring about the kingdom.

This was true on Good Friday when I humiliated myself in front of hundreds of people and this has been true all throughout my life. When I was not elected to be president of CCM, I found myself free to take a new position, one that I later found out was a much better fit for me and CCM; in Mexico, I was not able to do anything I planned on doing, but I experienced more minority and humility than I ever had in my life, arguably much more important things for me to learn at the time; and the resettlement fiasco, though painful for the whole parish, actually brought people together and taught me some invaluable lessons about leadership that I could not have learned any other way. Even when I have fallen short, even when things did not go as planned and the world would be quick to call something a failure, there was God, redeeming and transforming an experience into something life-giving.

For that reason, I would like to conclude this book by reflecting briefly on four experiences of failure I believe we all have, sharing the ways that each have challenged my life and how God has transformed each failure into success. This first post, written in 2014 shortly after the remodeling of the friary gym, addresses a topic that has haunted me most of my life: weakness.

Weight Room Theology

"No pain, no gain."

"If you can't outplay them, outwork them."

"It's all about who wants it more."

"The difference between the impossible and the possible lies in a person's determination."

"You gotta burn it to earn it"

"Pain is weakness leaving the body."

"Go big or go home."

"If you fail to prepare, you're prepared to fail."

As someone who has taken sports and athletic training very seriously my whole life, quotes like these really get me going. Even watching certain commercials make me want to jump off the couch and hit the weights. I can work harder. I can get better.

I can be great. There is within me a constant demand for progress and the belief that it is within the realm of my free will to achieve it (or not) based on the amount of effort I put in. Hard work pays off, as they say, and so I'm all about hard work.

And while most of us recognize that our free will is only one contributing factor to our success (along with our genetic makeup, social upbringing, and chance), I imagine that most of us buy into these weight-room mantras to some extent. We want to be in control. We want to think that we can determine our own future, that it is not some unchangeable characteristic of our biology that determines our life, but rather our dedication and innovation. Isn't that the American way? At the core of who we are, we are a people that upholds the freedom to make of ourselves what we can, that hard work should be rewarded with success.

I think that's really the crux of it: We are a people that believes that we are able to and should earn everything we have. We live with the notion that the world is a meritocracy, that those who work hard will be successful and those who are lazy or incompetent will be unsuccessful. In this world, everything is in our control. We can choose to work hard or not, but ultimately success is within our hands. When people hear that the actual greatest indicator of one's success is the social status of the family in which one is born, most want to reject this: The privileged want to think that they earned what they were given, and the poor want to believe that their situation can be changed if only they work hard enough. Everyone wants to be in control; everyone wants to believe that we can earn whatever we want.

It's no wonder, then, that weight-room mantras and motivational quotes pervade all aspects of our life, even our relationship with God. Without even realizing it, many of us have adopted a weight-room theology in which salvation is yet another task to be overcome by our will and earned by our hard work.

Can we really earn our salvation? Can we really work hard enough to deserve a place in heaven? Will any amount of innovation, creativity, or usefulness really make God love us? The answer to all three is clearly no. Because we are God's creation, made in God's image to reflect the divine aspect and to give everything we are back to our Creator, there is nothing we ever do above and beyond what is expected of us. God's grace to us is something that is freely given and undeserved. It is a true gift, something that is not as a result of our actions and does not warrant anything in return. God created us, Jesus became like us, and the Spirit now remains with us, not because of who we are, but because of who God is.

But that doesn't sit well with us type-A Americans, does it? We want to know that what we are doing means something, that we can overcome ourselves to assure the result we want. We allow a weight room theology to slip in. "If I say all my prayers every day, God will love me." "I followed all the rules of the Church, received every sacrament I could, and gave money to the poor." "I did something really bad. I need to do something to make up for it so God will forgive me." In each of these statements there is a desire to be in control, to convince God of our worthiness by doing good things. Isn't that a bit silly when we think about it, though? Surely we could never convince God of anything, and even if we could, there could never be a rule to follow or a deed to complete that would be enough.

So does that mean everything is for nought? If we can't earn salvation, what does it matter how we act? For our answer, let's look to the parable of the Great Feast (Matthew 22:1–14; Luke 14:15–24). In both versions, the great king sends out his servants to tell the invited guests that the banquet is ready. They did not pay to enter the banquet, nor is it implied that they did anything to deserve attendance. What do they do with such a gift? They choose not to come. Caught up with worldly concerns, they make excuses and turn down the free banquet. Enraged, the king sends out his servants to the streets, inviting anyone and everyone, including "the poor and the crippled, the blind and the lame," surely not people that earned a place at the table. This does not mean that nothing is expected of them, however. Noticing that one of the guests came without a wedding garment, a sign of repentance and changed heart (not to mention disrespectful to the host!), the king kicked him out with the others that chose not to accept the gift.

Even though it is up to God who ultimately gets invited to the feast, it is up to us whether or not we accept the invitation and show up with a heart open to conversion. It is an acceptance that we are not in control of our destiny, that no amount of hard work or merit could ever guarantee us a place before God. In the chapel, unlike the weight room, we rely not on our own strength to be great, for our strength is nothing on its own. Rather, it is when we are weak that we are strong, when we allow Christ to lift us up, to take our pain, to direct our lives, that Christ lives in us and we are truly strong.

One of the most important—and most annoying—stages everyone has to go through as they mature is proving that they can be independent from others. When I was not yet old enough to swim on my own, I *could* have put my floaties on and asked my parents to help, but I chose to jump in on my own and ended up flailing for help. When I saw a cool sparkler at a Fourth of July party, I *could* have let my mom hold it for me, but I decided to light it myself and ended up burning my hand. When I found myself lonely and outcast in high school, I *could* have talked to my dad, a teacher, or coach, but I opted to keep it to myself and ended up living with low self-esteem for years. Whether it is the constant "no" of a two-year-old, the "I can do it myself" of an eight-year-old, or the "leave me alone" of a teenager, help is often turned down just to prove to ourselves that we are independent...even when it is the thing we need most. Living on our own strength and refusing to accept that there are things we cannot do on our own, we certainly do find our independence, but we also found a lot of pain and heartache as well.

Living on our own strength is not all that it is cracked up to be.

As much as learning some level of independence is an important part of growing up, we often take this desire to its unhealthy extreme, forgetting a critical fact of life: No one is truly independent. In every success we have, there are always those who made it possible. In every defeat, there are always those around us reaching out to help, if only we would let them. We are not the determiners of our own fate, and as hard as it is to accept, there are simply things that are way outside of our control. Sometimes we succeed by chance. Other times, we fail despite doing everything right. The world is just too complicated, too difficult, and too unpredictable for us to believe that we can absolutely control even the smallest aspect of our lives, let alone the major issues of our day.

For this reason, it can certainly be comforting, at times, to buy into the mantras of the day and feel like life follows the rules of a Gatorade commercial—hard work always pays off and we are the authors of our own story. But can you imagine if the fate of the world actually *was* in our hands? Can you imagine if we truly *did* have to save ourselves? There are some days when I cannot even get out of bed without hitting the snooze button five times, let along saving myself from the evil and destruction of the world! Left to myself, I need help. I cannot do it on my own. I am weak.

Luckily for us, our God is all the strength we could ever need. Our God is the creator of the universe, the author of life, and the reason that everything remains in existence. There is no problem that God cannot solve, no fear that God cannot overcome, no weakness that God cannot make strong. This is the God, we remember, that took an unjust execution and turned it into salvation for all humankind. This is the God, of course, that was able to take my failed homily and turn it into a dramatic image of our faith. God is the only strength that we could ever need.

But there is a catch: God is only strong *for those who are truly weak.*

The great mystery of our faith—the truly countercultural and prophetic message of the kingdom found in the life of Jesus—is that God seeks out the lowly, not the successful. As Mary sings of God in her *Magnificat,* "He has cast down the mighty from their thrones, and has lifted up the humble. He has filled the hungry with good things, and the rich he has sent away empty" (Luke 1:52–53). God has no need for those who do not need him. Just like the child who says "No," "I can do it myself," and "leave me alone," God cannot be strength for those who believe that they need no more strength. It is only in weakness, in failing to be able to do it ourselves and failing to live up to the standards of our world, that God can be the strength that we need. Against the values of our world, there is no shame in being weak. All we have to do is ask for help.

For many, this is easy to accept. We know, of course, that we are not perfect, and most of us do not expect perfection out of ourselves. We have no problem admitting that we need God in our lives. But if we are *more* than just weak or "not perfect"? What if we find that our weakness is actually in doing things that we know that we should not do, things that God has specifically forbidden? What if our failures are not in our natural human limitations, but the failure of *sin*? There, it would seem, we have a different problem, and once again might find ourselves struggling with the despair of failure. *How can God love me if I am a sinner?* This next post, an adapted homily about the Rich Man and Lazarus (Luke 16:19–31) from my time in seminary, recalls a time when I fell very short of God's mark.

I Didn't Do Anything

"I didn't do anything."

That's what I said to the principal when I was called into her office in fourth grade. You see, there was a kid in my class that no one really liked. He was loud and immature, often dressed inappropriately and had bad hygiene, and was known for acting out, bullying others, and saying inappropriate things to the girls. He was a bully that no one liked...a very bad combination.

One day, things boiled over. At morning recess, he apparently touched one of the girls in our class and said something to her, and my friends didn't like that. Enough was enough. They planned to teach him a lesson. At lunch recess, they were going to corner him and beat him up, as they said. When lunch came, we all went out to recess, and three of the guys in my class started pushing him, calling him names. I think one of them even kicked him.

The kid didn't sustain any major injuries, just a scraped knee and a scratch above his eye, but it was a big deal in the school. The three students who had orchestrated the whole thing were called into the principal's office, but so was I along with a few other students. "I didn't do anything," I said. "It was ____ and ____ and ____. They were the ones who beat him up. I did not even touch him."

In my mind, I was innocent. My principal didn't think so. As she saw it, I knew something bad was going to happen, but I didn't stop it. Why didn't I say something? Why didn't I intervene? Why didn't I help him? Even though he was weird, even though he might have even brought it on himself, even though I may have suffered a bit myself for defending him, no one deserves to be treated that way. I had the power to do something, but didn't do anything.

In our Gospel passage today, the rich man finds himself in a similar situation. No doubt shocked to find himself in a place of torment while Lazarus is in the place of honor, you can almost hear him say, "But I didn't do anything. I didn't make him poor. I didn't steal from him. I didn't make him unclean." And maybe he didn't. But just like me in the fourth grade, the rich man knew Lazarus. He knew that he was suffering. I mean, c'mon, he was lying at his door! He probably needed to step over him to go out! Even though Lazarus was not the most desirable person in town, even though he was probably unclean and the rich man may have suffered for helping him, no one deserves to be treated that way. The rich man had the power to do something, but didn't do anything.

I think that is what's so powerful for us to remember today: Not doing anything is not amoral. Doing nothing does not free us from guilt. In life, there is no "pass"; we can't just opt out of acting... even doing nothing is something. It's why in the Confiteor, the act of contrition we say at Mass, we pray for God to forgive the sins of "What I have done, and what I have failed to do." Sometimes, what we don't do can have a tremendous effect on others, and can absolutely be sinful.

It doesn't take much to see this in our world. When we look at the world's problems, global epidemics of poverty, climate change, human trafficking, and so on, it's easy for us to say, "Well, I didn't do that." And maybe we didn't. But what we often don't realize is that we are in a position of privilege. If you are able to read this post, it's likely that you find yourself among the wealthiest 25 percent in the world. Wealth. Education. Civil liberties. Social status. Even just the knowledge that there are problems in the world that need fixing and the time to think about them is a privilege. In so many situations, we are the rich man facing Lazarus each day.

But it happens much closer to home. What about our friends and families? Here in this house as brothers, we often know what our brothers are going through. We know that they need help at times. Sometimes, it can be very easy, especially if it's a brother that we don't particularly like or even annoys us, to write him off and say, "He brought it on himself," or, "He's not my responsibility," or, "I didn't do anything." And likely we didn't. But that's not what's important here: There is a situation in which we are able to do something to build up the kingdom of God.

Because, in the end, whether it's our brother Lazarus or that poor boy in my fourth-grade class, it is not up to us to determine who is worthy and who is not. It is not we who grant dignity, and so it is not up to us to decide whom we should care for and whom we shouldn't. We may face a lot of people in need in our life, a lot of whom are very difficult to be around—you might even think about some people in this house. Who knows. One day, though, we will have to answer to Jesus for what we did and what we did not do. On that day, will we be able to say that we did something for our brothers and sisters in need, or will we be left with nothing to say except, "I didn't do anything"?

Personal pain and suffering is one thing, but letting someone down is a completely different feeling of defeat. One time in novitiate I borrowed the novice master's credit card to run some errands for the house. I went to a couple of different stores for the house, made a few personal stops of my own while I was out, and returned to the house. When I got back, I went to give him back his card but could not find it. Not in my wallet and not in the car, and having stopped too many places along the way to know where it might have been lost, I had the most uncomfortable experience of walking into his office and telling him the bad news. Initially greeting me with a smile, I watched his face slowly slump to the dreadful realization that was ahead of him: It was the house card, so he would soon have to change the automatic payments to dozens of services to match a replacement card number. Not the least bit angry at me, his depressing disappointment made me utterly sick. I had let him down.

Sin is like this feeling, except the person we are disappointing is God and the issue is over more than a stupid piece of plastic. *So, maybe a little more intense feeling.* With sin, we hold the guilt of not only letting someone down, we carry the fear that such an act could cost us our life. As Scripture tells us, the penalty for sin is death, and who is going to question God's judgment in such things? While the world may have forgotten the weight that sin places on our souls, this is not lost on the Christian. Letting God down, quite obviously, carries the worst possible consequences we can ever imagine. If we think about *that*, it is hard not to become utterly sick.

Of course, our God is not only all powerful; God's mercy surpasses anything we could ever imagine.

I caught my first glimpse of this when I was in college. I really wanted to live the Gospel as purely as I could and was becoming very frustrated with myself, not just because I was sinning (we're all sinners, right?) but with the consistency of the same sins. I went to confession three times in a month or two, and by the third time I was downright ashamed. I said, "Father, I am just so disappointed in myself. I committed the *same three sins* that I have confessed multiples times this semester." Sheepishly, I waited for his response, expecting some strict admonishment or disappointment matching my own. To my surprise, that is not what I got. The priest, equally as sheepish sounding, responded, "I'm really sorry, but you are going to have to remind me what they were. I do not hold on to these things."

He had forgotten.

In that moment, the gravity of God's mercy and the whole concept of absolution became clear to me. When I confessed my sins, showing contrition and a true resolve to live a better life, the guilt I carried with me did not just get wiped off or covered up, *it completely disappeared*. In God's eyes, I truly was forgiven. Not hidden, not ignored, *forgiven*. Gone forever.

I felt in that moment that God's mercy is not like our mercy that is able to hold on to grudges or remember past hurts; God's mercy is the purest form of forgiveness imaginable, found in the foundation of true love. Like the father of the prodigal son, when a sinner returns looking for forgiveness and asking for a place at the table, God is not concerned with punishment; there is no need for justice. All God can give is an overflowing of merciful love. The sacrament of confession—and every moment of contrition in the heart of a sinner—is a moment of joy for God.

But that is hard for us to accept. Working from what we know and knowing what *we* are capable of (and not capable of), there is always a part of us deep down that remains skeptical. Yes, God will forgive me. *But to what extent?* For those of us (everyone) who struggle to learn from our mistakes, who want with all our hearts to serve God perfectly and yet find ourselves repeatedly and defiantly disobeying God's desires, we cannot help but think of ourselves as stiff-necked, hardheaded people. Our sin, we come to realize, is not just the occasional and one-time mishap that we learn from and put behind us. This post, written just before Lent in 2017, calls to mind that unfortunate stubborn part of our nature.

Learning My Lesson...Again

For nearly six years I have lived in a community of religious men seeking to live humbly and serve others. I have been to workshops, heard lectures, gone on retreats, prayed for countless hours, and really, just lived this life for more than two thousand days. You would think that I'd have learned a few lessons in that time.

Apparently not.

A couple of weeks ago, I came home for lunch to find a mess in the kitchen: There was peanut butter everywhere. If that sounds like a strange statement, it's because it is. I don't know who did it or how it happened without them noticing, but there was peanut butter on the faucet of the sink, the counter, the cabinet handle, the refrigerator, and the bag of bread. Presumably, someone used the peanut butter, got some on his hand without realizing it, and spread it to everything he touched.

Ultimately, that's irrelevant, though. My first reaction was not "how…" it was "ah, hell no!" I took one look at the mess and said, as I have been known to do over the past six years, "Not my problem." I was not going to deal with this mess. I was in a hurry, had my own lunch to make…whoever did this—and all the rest of the friars—could come home and see what a jerk he was and clean it himself. Not doing it.

Fast forward fifteen seconds.

There I was, having leaned up against the counter I had just complained about, with peanut butter on my habit. Ugh. This is not going to come out easily. Initially even angrier at whomever had left the mess, I found myself feeling really stupid moments later. Had I simply taken fifteen seconds to get a rag and cleaning spray, the kitchen would have been clean and my habit would not smell like lunch. Was it really that big a deal to clean up after someone else?

The answer is no. And really, the answer is always no. As much as what the other person did is disrespectful, rude, lazy, and inexcusable, a passive-aggressive response is never the answer. Letting myself get angry and handling the issue indirectly— simply leaving the mess in hopes that it will annoy others or send a message to the person who did it—is not the way to resolve an issue; it's the way I get peanut butter on myself.

Hmm... How symbolic. It's almost as if when we try to avoid an issue, choosing to "send a message" rather than simply talking with the person with whom we have a problem, we end up carrying the mess ourselves without them even knowing it.

Naturally, this is but an insignificant kitchen situation, but really, how different is it from the serious issues of life? So often in my life I find myself frustrated with something someone else has done, how they've treated me, or what they stand for. How easy it would be to simply address the issue head on, grab a rag, and get rid of it: "Hey, can we talk about something that's bothering me?" But no. I prefer to hold on to my resentment, let myself get angry without them knowing anything is wrong, and hope that they get the message from my subtle slights and distancing myself from them. That'll show them what they did.

Or it won't.

Sometimes, it doesn't matter how "religious" we are or how much we know, the simplest lessons need to be repeated from time to time; sometimes we need to go back to basics. Luckily for us Christians, the liturgical year offers us a built-in mechanism for doing just that. As we pass from season to season—especially as we yearly approach Lent—we return to lessons and teachings that we've heard again and again, hoping each year that some will stick for the long haul. It's a chance to look at our lives and reflect, to take a step back, return to what we know and ask ourselves if that's what we do. As I have found out over the past six years, and as I was reminded in the kitchen just a few weeks ago, our faith is not the exclusive domain of sacred spaces and buildings: It is something that is lived (and learned) in the ordinary, mundane, messes-in-the-kitchen situations of life. One day, if we're lucky, we'll all learn our lesson.

The funny thing about this post, and really, the reason I wrote it in the first place, was because I had literally written about the same topic the year before. Living in a different house at the time, I wrote about how someone left the bathroom a mess, and rather than cleaning it, I left it and went to the other bathroom, only to find out later that the reason it had been so messy was because the brother was seriously ill. My take away—again, just a year before writing this post above—was that sometimes we need to have humility to do things that we do not think we should need to do, that serving our brothers and sisters always needs to be our highest priority, and that choosing to send a message often works, but the message we send when we act this way is "We're all in this alone so don't expect any help from me."¹

Yeah. What is that they say about practicing what you preach?

Unfortunately, this is not an isolated case of failing to live up to Gospel life, nor do I think that I am alone in this experience. The fact of the matter is that *we all fall short of our Christian values.* How many times have we said "love one another" and then immediately turned around and ignored someone in need? How many times have we said "prayer is the foundation of our life" and then gone days without spending time with God? How many times have we said, "I am going to quit that bad habit" and then fallen right back into it days later? How many times have we known exactly what God wants—and wanted to do it ourselves—and gone off and done something else? Oh, what a stiff-necked, hard-headed people we are. No doubt, if we were all as bad at our jobs as we are at living up to the ideals of Christianity, we would probably be fired so quickly and often that we would not want to try working anymore.

It is because of this that I have wanted to give up at times. Knowing that God had forgiven me time and again, I have found myself multiple times in my life too ashamed to even go to confession. *How can I honestly say that I am contrite and do not want to sin again when I have confessed these same sins countless times before?* One time in particular, I got it in my head that I had to prove it to myself and God that I was serious this time. (Already, after reading the first part of this chapter you can see that this is not going to end well.) I identified the three most burdensome sins in my life, and I told myself that I could not go to confession until I had gone two months without committing any of them.

More than six months later, I had still not gone to confession, and each one was killing me.

When I finally went, I told the priest this story. Sarcastically, he responded, "And how'd that work out for ya?" Obviously, it had been a disaster, as he already knew. And how could I have expected it to go any differently? Not only was I acting like my childhood self, demanding that I be able to do something by myself without asking for help, I was withholding from myself the very mercy and grace I needed to overcome my weakness. I had let my sin deceive me into thinking that I should do something other than go directly to God for help, deciding that it was smarter to deal with my sin alone than to just swallow my pride and just ask God to be God. Even though I had failed in the same ways yet again, the solution was no different than before: Go to God and ask for forgiveness. No matter what we have done, God wants nothing more than for us to return to him.

How difficult this is for us to grasp. How difficult it is for us to understand that even repetitive, habitual sin, even when we continue to make the same mistakes over and over, even then God is ready to forgive us. As Pope Francis has said on multiple occasions but it always worth repeating, "God never tires of forgiving us; we are the ones who tire of seeking his mercy." No matter how often we fall short—and we will a lot, even if we are vowed religious and engage in pastoral ministry—the only thing ever preventing us from receiving God's mercy is ourselves. We just have to ask. While sin may always be a problem in our lives, something that we will never fully avoid or get over, we know that God's mercy will always prevail.

So even sin, for many people, is not the overwhelming failure that stops us in our tracks and demoralizes us. Full of guilt when we fall short and wishing we were better, some recognize, once again, that we will never be perfect this side of death, and so we can happily rely on God's mercy to forgive and save us from ourselves.

But what about that final weakness? What about the weakness of all weaknesses, the fear above all fears? What about *death*? They say that with taxes it is the only thing completely unavoidable, and for tax-exempt religious like me, that means it is the only thing I can truly count on in life: One day, my body and mind will cease to function, and the "me" as you know it will be no more. That, it would seem, is the ultimate failure of life. And it terrifies most.

In my opinion, there is no more important question in our whole life of faith and ministry than what we think about death and thus, how we approach it. This final post, written last year while on my internship, offers my own struggle with that looming reality, and the inevitable process leading up to it: getting old.

No Matter the Age

Upon turning seventy years old last week, one of our friars took the opportunity at Mass to share some words of wisdom and a beautiful prayer about what the experience of getting "old" is like. Using the words of Pierre Teilhard de Chardin, he said something to the effect of, "as the body begins to break and weaken, filling up with holes, one finds room for God they never had before." It was from the heart, insightful, and highly appropriate.

Or so I thought.

After concluding Mass, a parishioner approached him, agitated at what he had said. "You're not old! I'm seventy-eight and I still do so much. Do you think I'm old?!" While the friar was simply using the word as an objective category, "someone who is closer to death than baptism," as he said, the parishioner took the word to have an offensive undertone: Something that is "old" is less-capable, out-of-date, and undesirable.

It's a situation that I have been in many times in my life as a friar. Being the youngest friar in the province, I learned very quickly that what I considered "young" and "old" were often not what others did, and that using such words was to be done with extreme caution, if ever at all. Despite being a senior citizen, sixty-five was not "old" to a seventy-year-old. Despite being the average age of death, seventy five was not "old" to an eighty-year-old, and so on. Depending on who I'm talking to, someone who is forty, fifty, even sixty can be considered "young," and you don't dare call them otherwise.

You can guess what that frame of reference does to someone

in my position. At twenty-seven years old, having entered at twenty-two, I am the youngest professed friar in our province... and can never forget it. "Oh my God you're so young!" is a phrase I hear from parishioners and friars alike on a regular basis. For five years, it has been my minority status, the underrepresented category in our Order and Church that defines me, making me the unofficial spokesperson, expert, and representative for all things youthful. Because the friars are aging in this country, I am and probably will be "young" in this line of work far longer than if I were to do anything else.

Which is fine. Hooray. Outside of the occasional question of my maturity, being "young" is a great thing. It's the reason that seventy-eight-year-olds still think of themselves that way and refuse to use the word "old." It's the reason that Bob Dylan and Alphaville sang songs about it, why we have so much nostalgia for our youth, why it takes some people a decade to move on after college. Being "young" is what we want and being "old" is terrible. Right?

What I want to suggest in this post, and why I have the words "young" and "old" in quotes throughout, is that these words are generic terms that do not adequately reflect the human experience nor do they point us to what is really important.

As someone who has been branded with the title of "young" over the past five years, I can't help but recognize the irony of the fact that I have come to recognize my own age and mortality in that same time period. At twenty-two, when I became the "youngest in the province," I played my last-ever competitive baseball game. I reached an age in which the best of something was behind me. At twenty-four, being the "youngest novice in the country," I tore my shoulder and was told that I would have to begin exercising in a different way. I became physically unable to do something I once could. At twenty-seven, as parishioners can't believe that I'm old enough to be a friar, I notice that the small cut on my face from shaving has become a permanent scar, the stray and occasional grey hair has become a dozen fixed features of my scalp, and my one eye sags a little bit when I smile. My body is shifting from growth to decline. Despite being so "young," I can't help but feel "old" compared to how I used to be.

Am I "old" then? Aren't I still "young"? The obvious answer is that these terms are meant to be relative and only make sense in comparison to something else: I am old compared to the students at Immaculata Elementary School but quite young compared to my formators and provincial leadership. But I don't think that is what offends people at church or drives people to want to be "forever young." No, the problem is that we associate being "young" with life, vibrancy, and potential, whereas we associate being "old" with weakness, decay, and the past. Despite the fact that youth comes with its tremendous detriments (immaturity, doubt, lack of experience) and that increased age comes with its tremendous benefits (wisdom, confidence, identity), we somehow only remember the things we used to do but now can't, rather than all of the things we couldn't do but now can.

Why such pessimism? I can't speak for everyone, but I have a theory for most: We fear our own death more than we think. With everything that changes, diminishes, gets weaker, or disappears, we are reminded that there will come a day when we are a shadow of the person we once were; with everything that we lose, we are reminded that there will come a day when we lose it all. The little things we lose—the color of our hair, the quickness of our mind, the strength in our step—do not bother us in themselves. Who cares about a few grey hairs? It's what they represent that gets us. Loss. Diminishment. Irrelevancy. Death.

That's the problem with the categories we use: No matter the age, we all experience death and loss. It's not a binary system in which one goes from "young" to "old" overnight, from a period of growth to decline as if we're two different people. No matter the age, we are all confronted with the fact that the past is gone, that what we once knew and loved will not last forever. All things must come to an end.

So to speak.

While all of us have an innate fear of the unknown, difficulty handling loss, and uneasiness about death, we as Christians know at our very core that death is not the end, that loss is not the final note. It is precisely from death that we receive new life; it is from our pain, loss, and weakness that we find relief, gain more than we had, and know that Christ is strong in us. In an ultimate sense, we know that our death from this world will be made new with the resurrection, and we will rise with Christ on the last day.

But it's more than that and sooner than that. With every loss that we experience throughout our years, there is the sadness of saying goodbye to something we loved, but also room to welcome something new to love. Leaving college was sad... but starting a career is exciting. Not being able to play baseball anymore was devastating...but taking up a new hobby of golf is invigorating. Saying goodbye to the people we love is tragic... but finding the time and need to love others in their place is a life-giving opportunity. With every loss comes new life. It is in that understanding that I understand very clearly what my Franciscan brother meant to share at Mass last week: Sometimes, in the weak moments when all we seem to know are the holes of what used to be, we find that we have more room for God's work than we ever had before. I tell you, that is a lesson to learn, no matter the age.

And that is where I am going to end.

As unconventional as it may seem to end a book that is meant to be inspiring on the topic of failure and death, the fact of the matter is that Christianity is unconventional. The values of the world are not the values of our faith. As much as we might want to avoid the topic—heck, as much as I have spent my entire life *denying that it even exists*—the very essence of our faith and the foundation of who we are as disciples of Christ ministering in the world rests on how we understand and accept failure in our lives. No matter how "good" we are and no matter how much conviction we have, we *will* find ourselves weak; we *will* sin; we *will* refuse to change; and we absolutely *will* die one day. Learning to be a disciple of Christ and a minister to the world is not about hiding from these things, denying they exist, or trying to overcome them ourselves. No, truly *saying "yes" to God* means accepting that God is the only one who can overcome these things in our lives.

When we are weak, God offers strength.

When we are sinful, God offers forgiveness.

When we are hard of heart, God offers patience.

When we are dying, God offers eternal life.

I joined the friars because I wanted to do something with my life: I wanted to change the world. With so much around me in chaos, with so much yearning for greater meaning in life, I decided to devote my life to being that answer. I had two hands and a big heart, and with God on my side, nothing was impossible.

Of course, I had it all wrong. As I enter fully into this life six years later, solemnly professing that I will remain a friar for as long as I live, I know now that it is not my strength that the world needs, *it is my weakness*. The world does not need Casey Cole—nor does it need anyone else—to be its savior; it needs people who are willing to get out of the way, accepting that they cannot do anything on their own so to let Jesus Christ be the truest and fullest strength the world needs. I am a Franciscan Friar, living out my primary call to be a disciple of Jesus Christ, because I want nothing more for my life than to make him present in everything I do.

This is the reason I discern.

This is the reason I pray.

This is the reason I live in community.

This is the reason I seek to be lesser.

This is the reason I work to be whatever the world needs.

And this is why I leave you with a question: What does being a disciple of Jesus Christ mean to you? There is no singular, correct path God has laid out for us among the infinite number of incorrect ones; there is only the call that we devote ourselves fully to the one who gives everything to us. How will you answer that call?

About the Author

Casey Cole, OFM, is a vowed religious in the Order of Friars Minor, commonly known as the Franciscans. He has a degree in religious studies with a minor in poverty studies from Furman University. In August 2017, he professed his final vows within the Order of Friars Minor. He is in training to be ordained a priest, currently studying theology at the Catholic Theological Union in Chicago. His videos and blog can be found at BreakingInTheHabit.org.